Dennis Nilsen - The Necrophile Civil Servant

Mason Ryan

Other books by Mason Ryan:

Everything You Always Wanted To Know About Serial Killers (But Were Afraid To Ask)

The 100 Deadliest Serial Killers

The 100 Deadliest Female Serial Killers

Contents

PROLOGUE

The year is 1983. Margaret Thatcher is unstoppable after the victorious Falklands conflict. The Cold War and nuclear paranoia prevails. A young man named Jeffrey Dahmer is still a year or so shy of taking a job at a chocolate factory. Dr Harold Shipman has a flourishing surgery and recently appeared on the ITV documentary show World in Action sagely venturing forth on medical matters. The Yorkshire Ripper no longer lives in Bradford. His new address is Broadmoor Hospital - where jovial celebrity fundraiser Jimmy Saville has his own key. The original Star Wars trilogy has yet to be concluded. Roger Moore is James Bond. Larry Holmes is the world heavyweight boxing champion. There are four television channels and they all stop broadcasting near midnight. Kajagoogoo and Men at Work wage battle for the top of the British singles chart.

In Muswell Hill, a 37 year-old civil servant named Dennis Nilsen slumps into a chair under claustrophobic sloped ceilings. He's back in the tiny attic flat again after a bizarre midnight plumbing mission. Dennis Nilsen isn't sure of too much lately but one thing is certain. He's no plumber. The faint aroma of mothballs hangs in the air and a cold February night chills the room. The windows are always open. Dennis Nilsen is a fresh air fiend - for reasons that will soon become perfectly understandable.

This is a tatty and dismal place to live. This is where it all ends. Des, as the world at large knows this man, is a sardonic and somewhat mysterious character even to his few friends. He's a former soldier and army cadet. Briefly a beat bobby and police officer. Union rep. A trained chef. Recruitment interviewer at the Jobcentre. A loner. Music lover. Dog lover. An advocate of gay liberation. Stephen King lookalike. Socialist. Big drinker (Bacardi and rum in particular). Aficionado of the fried egg sandwich. Champion of the underdog. Lover of cowboy films. A son and a brother. Oh, and he's also a necrophile and a serial killer.

Definitions of sanity and insanity hit a brick wall when confronted with Des. He is calm and cogent. He seems rational and quite intelligent in conversation. He doesn't seem dangerous or insane at all. He also has a human head in his tea chest. A pair of severed legs in a cupboard. Body parts under the sink. For many months now Des has been boiling human heads on his rusty hob ring and stripping the flesh off to flush down the toilet. No back garden anymore you see. Not like Melrose Avenue. It was much easier then. Des would throw the remains on a bonfire with tyres and crush the bones with a rake.

Cranley Gardens is different. Three flights of stairs. No garden. Nosey neighbours. Did he move into this attic flat because he thought it would stop him? You would have to be completely insane to keep on killing people in a place where you had no way to dispose of the bodies wouldn't you? Des thought about this as he sat in the chair. Cranley Gardens hadn't stopped him. Only prison would stop him now. Maybe it was for the best. Des felt a strange sense of relief. Time was almost up. Maybe he'd wanted to be caught all along. He was surprised to have come this far...

In terms of statistics, Dennis Nilsen is generally regarded to Britain's second most prolific serial killer after Harold Shipman. It is open to question though on whether or not this is actually the case. Nilsen and other serial killers have unverified victims so the true tallies are difficult to know for certain. One thing is clear though - Dennis Nilsen was very prolific over a short period of time. It is terrifying to think of how many people he might potentially have killed if he hadn't been caught. If Dennis Nilsen had been able to drive he probably would have got away with his crimes for much longer and killed many more people. With a car, Nilsen would have been able to dispose of remains in woods or even rivers. If Dennis Nilsen was American he probably would have ended up in the electric chair.

Serial killers are, by their very nature, all odd, but even by the standards of serial killers Dennis Nilsen was pretty weird. A number of notorious serial killers have indulged in necrophilia but Nilsen took this grisly hobby to absurd lengths. Nilsen would put a dead body in a chair next to him and watch television with it. He would talk to dead people as if they were still alive. Nilsen would even sit down with a corpse and have dinner with it. Nilsen did this for about five years before he essentially doomed himself by blocking up his drain with human flesh. If he'd been the villain in an episode of Columbo, Nilsen would have posed no challenge whatsoever to the raincoated detective. Dennis Nilsen was definitely no criminal mastermind. In fact, Nilsen didn't really seem to care whether he would be caught or not. His actions strongly suggest that he wanted to be captured in the end.

When the disturbing and shocking crimes of Nilsen came to light, the police and the media were surprised when they clapped eyes on the man who was responsible for them. This was not a darkly charismatic lunatic or a feral outsider straight out of serial killer central casting. Dennis Nilsen was, well, rather dull. He was a very dour and dry sort sort of man. He worked in a Jobcentre and wore the same shirt every day. Dennis Nilsen was surprisingly boring. When he went on trial, court reporters were astonished by how ordinary Dennis Nilsen looked. They had been expecting a monster but the quiet bespectacled man sitting in court didn't really conform to their expectations. Nilsen did have a sullen darkness about him though. He looked like a man who had never smiled in his life.

A lot of serial killers pointlessly maintain they are innocent - despite the considerable evidence weighted against them. A lot (though not all) of serial killers also dislike discussing their deadly and awful crimes in detail. None of this applied to Dennis Nilsen. Nilsen confessed straight away and was more than happy to discuss his crimes in great depth with anyone willing to listen to him. Nilsen actually seemed to enjoy his status as a notorious serial killer. Though his fame was the worst kind of fame imaginable, Nilsen seemed to take a strange pride in the spotlight he had been afforded thanks to his harrowing and perplexing crimes. He was sort of like the serial killer version of Rupert Pupkin from Martin Scorsese's The King of Comedy. Nilsen thought it was much better to be notorious necrophile serial killer for a night than a forgotten nobody for a lifetime.

Nilsen never seemed to indicate any sense of shame about his crimes or the twisted and tragic path his life had taken. It's hard to say if he ever felt remorse for his actions and victims - though he claimed he did. Are serial killers really capable of human emotions? You probably wouldn't be a serial killer in the first place if you had a range of basic human emotions. These normal human feelings are the safety valve that make the vast majority of people incapable of awful deeds. It was certainly plausible that Nilsen had a sense of regret but he wasn't really capable of empathy for the relatives of his victims or a sincere sense of sorrow for what he had done. Nilsen did genuinely wish that things had turned out differently but only for selfish reasons.

Dennis Nilsen killed all those men because he knew the connection he had with them was fleeting. He knew they would leave him and he didn't want that to happen. Nilsen once wrote - 'I had always held within me a fear of emotional rejection and failure. Nobody ever really got close to me. There was never a place for me in the scheme of things. My inner emotions could not be expressed, and this led me to the alternative of a retrograde and deepening imagination. I had become a living fantasy on a theme in dark endless dirges.'

Nilsen's inability to cope with rejection became fused with a lifelong yearning for necrophilia. If he killed these men then they would never be able to leave him and he would also have complete control over them. Nilsen could fufil his two greatest fantasies through murder. Until such time as decomposition took place that is. When this happened, Nilsen's necrophilia fantasies evaporated and gave way to more traditional serial killer headaches like having to get rid of bodies and body parts.

Nilsen was a slightly atypical sort of serial killer in that he killed all of his victims in his homes. So he ended up in two small flats that became festooned with decomposing bodies and body parts. Nilsen would boil heads on his hob rings and saw bodies in half in his kitchen. By any rational criteria, Dennis Nilsen was completely and utterly insane. And yet, he still went to work throughout this period. He didn't seem insane in the slightest to the people who worked in the same office.

Dennis Nilsen also spent eleven years in the armed forces. He was then a police constable with the Met. It's not unheard of at all for serial killers to be former soldiers or police officers but that largely (if not exclusively) tends to be an American phenomenon. It is somewhat novel for a modern British serial killer to be a former soldier and police officer like Nilsen was. Nilsen was also unusual in the introspection and naval gazing he applied to his life and crimes. Rarely has a serial killer spent so much time trying to diagnose themselves.

Dennis Nilsen wrote thousands of pages of autobiographical notes while he was in prison. The only British serial killer to rival Nilsen when it came to pomposity and self-importance was (his fellow Scot) Ian Brady. What was the end result of Nilsen's furious writing? Did he ever manage to deduce how he turned out the way he did? Well, not really. How can you ever really explain why someone would sit watching television with a corpse or boil human heads on their hob ring while they listen to the radio?

You might suggest loneliness made Nilsen do these terrible things but that barely feels like a satisfactory answer. Most people feel lonely at times but they don't become Dennis Nilsen as a consequence. The most salient actor in Nilsen's crimes was necrophilia. Nilsen was addicted to the power he

felt when he had mastery of a dead person. He was acting out
his darkest fantasy. The fantasy could never be permanent
though. The bodies would inevitably decay and smell. They
had to be disposed of. Nilsen then had to kill again to begin the
fantasy afresh. It was what you might describe as a classic
example of a vicious circle.

THE RAFT OF THE MEDUSA

Dennis Andrew Nilsen was born on the 23rd of November 1945 in Fraserburgh, Aberdeenshire. Nilsen always hated the name Dennis. This was why he liked to be called Des instead. Dennis Nilsen took on the nickname 'Des' because he felt this made him seem more likeable, informal, and friendly. An unquantifiable number of people have a lingering sense of dislocation concerning their origins. These people tend to feel as if they accidentally stepped out of an elevator on the wrong floor and have been desperately trying to find that elevator again ever since. Maybe there was a mistake at the hospital and the wrong family took them home? So it was with Dennis Nilsen. His family gradually became strangers to him as he got older.

Even at a tender age, Dennis Nilsen was quite sure - thank you very much - that he didn't want to spend his life in Fraserburgh working in a fish canning factory. Fraserburgh was not quite the end of the world but it sure felt like it to Dennis Nilsen. Nilsen would inevitably go on to become the most famous person to hail from this small fishing town. Tough luck on that one Fraserburgh but you don't get too many world famous necrophile serial killers.

Fraserburgh has a small population of around 13,000 today but it was even less than that when Nilsen was a child in the days before EU migrants. Fraserburgh is the biggest shellfish port in Scotland and has one of the oldest golf courses in the world. Dennis Nilsen described his childhood in Fraserburgh as drab and monochrome. He felt as if he was trapped in a dull black and white film where nothing ever happened. Des would lose himself in the bleakly beautiful coast and take long lonely walks to nowhere in particular. This was his means of escape. Whatever he was looking for on these endless rambles he never found.

Dennis Nilsen's father was a Norwegian soldier who came to Scotland in 1940 during the war. His name was Olav Magnus Moksheim until he took the surname Nilsen. Olav didn't stick around for very long though. Dennis Nilsen's mother Elizabeth then married a man named Andrew Scott when Dennis Nilsen was three years-old. Dennis didn't like Scott very much (Andrew Scott was alleged to be strict and quite stern). Dennis Nilsen's mother had some more children with Andrew Scott and this made Dennis Nilsen feel sidelined and alienated. He said he always felt completely abandoned by his real father.

Dennis Nilsen would later say that his new stepfather was the source of much of his anger and frustration. 'In those days I could hate Adam Scott very easily. I was, I suppose, very jealous of him having a relationship with and the attention of my mother. I sometimes felt that we, the Nilsen kids, were an impediment to her fulfilment in her new life and family. I was a very lonely and turbulent child. I inhabited my own secret world full of ideal and imaginary friends. Nature had mismatched me from the flock.'

The relationship between Des and his mother was never especially close. Dennnis Nilsen would later say that he never had anything in common with his mother at all and this always made the relationship difficult. Although his mother apparently did her best to maintain contact and communication with Dennis throughout his life, once he became an adult he regarded her with indifference at best. In the end he stopped opening her letters and never went back to Fraserburgh - even for a brief visit. When it came down to it, Dennis Nilsen just didn't seem to like his mother very much. He didn't really care in the end whether they had any contact or not.

The extended family around Des was old fashioned and strict. Dennis Nilsen said his grandmother was very religious and would preposterously lecture him on the 'evils' of things like music and dancing. As you might imagine, it wasn't exactly a barrel of laughs growing up in this family. Dennis Nilsen said that his family was cold and not tactile. He believes this played a part in him always feeling detached and aloof in society. Nilsen was always a very introspective and introverted person.

There was a history of mental health problems in the Nilsen family. Dennis Nilsen had a great aunt who spent most of her life in a mental asylum. In the run up to his trial for multiple murders decades later, Dennis Nilsen was (to the exasperation of his lawyers) strangely reluctant to accept a plea of diminished responsibility - despite the insistence of his legal team that this was the most pragmatic and obvious course of action. This was a rather bizarre situation. A necrophile serial killer who doesn't want anyone to think he might be mad! It may be that the memory of his great aunt still lingered and left Dennis Nilsen with a lifelong fear of ending up in a mental asylum or hospital himself.

Mental illness also seemed to dog Nilsen's mother when he was a child. Elizabeth was prone to violent mood swings where she would suddenly - without much warning - begin shouting at her children for no apparent reason. This suggests bipolar disorder - which used to be known as manic depression. As a consequence of these mood swings, Dennis Nilsen clearly found it difficult to warm to his mother. It's somewhat difficult to have rose tinted memories of someone when most of those memories involve the person in question shouting at you.

Dennis Nilsen (predictably you might say) described himself as an unhappy and brooding child. He enjoyed reading horror stories when he was young as a means of escape. Nilsen said he was painfully aware at a young age of the tension between fantasy and reality. He loved the escapism of cinema and always found harsh reality to be a crushing disappointment. We all prefer fantasy to reality but most of us are aware of the fact that we must ultimately accept reality and make the best of it. This was something that Nilsen never quite came to terms with. Nilsen's nightmarish attempts to live in a dark fantasy of his own making would later have tragic consequences for a number of victims.

Nilsen was a fan of film stars like Gary Cooper and Jimmy Stewart when he was a child. It seemed to be a great disappointment to Dennis Nilsen that screen heroes were confined to the screen and didn't exist in real life. Even in the midst of his later murders, with body parts scattered around his flat, he would be drawn to cowboy films if one appeared on television and stop what he was doing (which was usually something very gruesome and grisly) to watch. Cinema was his ultimate form of escape as a child.

Dennis Nilsen famously said his grandfather was the most important and reliable person in his life and that he never recovered from the death of this relative. Andrew Whyte was a fisherman and had the closest bond with the young Dennis of anyone in the family. Grandfather and grandson would take walks together and spent a lot of time in one another's company. Andrew Whyte has therefore assumed a mythical sort of role in the story of Dennis Nilsen. Andrew Whyte was the only person who could have saved Dennis Nilsen but through his death he ended up unwittingly creating Dennis Nilsen. This is the bare bones thesis put forward by several writers - not least Dennis Nilsen himself.

Of the death of his grandfather, Dennis Nilsen wrote - 'My troubles started there. It blighted my personality permanently. I have spent all my emotional life searching for my grandfather and in my formative years no one was there to take his place.' In his book about Dennis Nilsen, Brian Masters offered the theory that the sight of his dead grandfather left Dennis Nilsen with a sense that death and love were as one and connected. This, according to the thesis, sowed the seeds for the tragic dysfunction and awful path of Dennis Nilsen's later life.

Dennis Nilsen had an obsession (a fetish one might say) with death. He saw a beautiful serenity and peace in death. He was appalled at the thought that dead people were buried in the ground. Nilsen had a fantasy of preserving and celebrating corpses as if they were still alive. Andrew Whyte looms large then in the genesis of Dennis Nilsen. The sight of the dead, serene, and beloved Andrew Whyte in his coffin is the catalyst for the notorious Dennis Nilsen. Well, maybe. Andrew Whyte's relationship with Dennis Nilsen was more complicated than that. It was much darker than the surface gloss.

In his 'memoir', Dennis Nilsen said that his grandfather once stuck one of his fingers up Nilsen's bottom. In this prison penned autobiography, Dennis Nilsen describes his supposedly beloved grandfather as a 'tepid paedophile' but not a 'threatening' one. Nilsen makes it pretty clear that his grandfather sexually abused him yet doesn't seem to be aware the gravity of this. He almost writes as if it was no big deal. The dysfunction and strangeness of Nilsen carries over into his writing. He is literally the last person in the world qualified to diagnose himself.

Dennis Nilsen had a younger biological sister named Sylvia. Sylvia got married at sixteen and emigrated to Canada. In his 'memoir', Nilsen seemed to suggest he indecently fondled his siblings when they were all children. Dennis Nilsen is said to have had a bad relationship with his older biological brother Olaf because Olaf (who had obviously deduced the sexuality of his brother from a very young age) didn't like the fact that Nilsen was gay. Dennis Nilsen's brother is alleged to have once said (with Dennis Nilsen very much in mind) that "Fraserburgh isn't a very good place for a poofter." Dennis Nilsen's brother Olaf used to infuriate him by calling Nilsen 'hen'. Hen is a Scottish slang word for woman. It is believed that Dennis Nilsen never spoke to his brother Olaf again after 1972 - around the time that he moved to London.

Dennis Nilsen realised that he was gay at a very young age. He said that this created a feeling of tension and alienation because he both grew up and lived as an adult at a time when being gay was still actually against the law. Dennis Nilsen said that Fraserburgh was full of religious 'bigots' when he was growing-up. As he became increasingly aware that he was gay, he realised that this might not be the greatest place in the world for a gay person to live. Dennis Nilsen liked to think of himself as bisexual when he was young - though this wasn't the case. He couldn't bring himself to admit that he was 100% gay at first.

Nilsen seemed to suggest in his autobiographical writing that he first knew he was gay at school when the sight of the other boys in their PE kits excited him. His sexuality was something that he found difficult to accept as a child and teenager. The fifties and sixties were a difficult time to be gay - especially if one lived in a small old fashioned sort of place where everyone seemed to know each other. Nilsen also spent part of his childhood in a village named Strichen. Strichen is about eight miles from Fraserburgh. Less than a thousand people lived in Strichen and Nilsen found it a dull place. Years later, Strichen would become best known for being the home of the politician Alex Salmond.

When he was a child, Dennis Nilsen claimed that he saw a boy who bullied him at school being pulled out to sea and apparently drowning. Nilsen said this image always stayed with him. It gave him a tremendous sense of excitement and satisfaction to see the boy being dragged out to sea. Dennis Nilsen also claimed that he nearly drowned in a childhood accident when he was nine years-old. He said that he was rescued by a boy who seemed to have a sexual interest in him. This event (if true) would obviously have had a profound effect on Nilsen. One must remember though that Dennis Nilsen was never the most reliable narrator of his own life. Fantasy and reality were always blurred in the memory of Dennis Nilsen.

When he was growing-up in the fishing port, Nilsen said he once joined the search for a local man who had gone missing. According to this story, Dennis Nilsen and a friend supposedly found the man's body on a riverbank. Some people have understandably cast doubt on some of Nilsen's claims about his childhood. With a man like Dennis Nilsen it is not always easy to separate fact from fantasy. Serial killers in general are never the best people to tell their own story. They embellish and subtract. They add in fictional details and mask genuine ones. Nilsen seemed to be at pains to make his childhood more melodramatic and tragic than it actually was.

The warning signs that one might become a serial killer are generally held (though of course not everyone agrees with these generalisations) to be early incidents of cruelty to animals, pyromania, head injuries, indecent exposure, prolonged bed wetting, hallucinations, theft, and coming from alcoholic families. Most serial killers develop a cold personality at a young age. They are sociopaths. Sociopaths lack a sense of responsibility or a social conscience. They are prone to antisocial behaviour. They can then tilt into becoming a psychopath.

How many of these 'warning signs' applied to Dennis Nilsen? Well, as far as we can see, none of them. * Dennis Nilsen's mother said that he was a sensitive child who would care for injured animals. He was later a famously a dog lover. Nilsen did not wet the bed, he was not an arsonist or teenage criminal, he suffered no head injuries, had no incidents of indecent exposure, and did not come from an alcoholic or drug addicted family. Although he always painted a stark picture of his childhood, Nilsen's early years were far from nightmarish or full of portents of his future. Many children have had tougher or more distressing childhoods than Dennis Nilsen and turned out to be decent, worthwhile adults. At the very least, they didn't become necrophile serial killers.

Dennis Nilsen might not have wet the bed or set fire to the local church but, as we have seen, incidents of incest and sexual abuse were not strangers to his young life. He was always plagued by dark sexual thoughts concerning death. Nilsen said that from a fairly young age all of his sexual fantasies were about dead people or people who were restrained and couldn't move. A study once found that 86% of serial killers had sexual fantasies like this. Ownership and total control of a person is a common fantasy that fuels the depraved activities of the worst serial killers. As a young man, Dennis Nilsen would smear himself with white makeup and talcum powder and pretend he was dead. He said he found this erotic. Many serial killers love the thought of having a helpless sexual victim at their mercy and you don't get more helpless than being dead.

As a young man, Nilsen became obsessed with a painting called The Raft of the Medusa by the French Romantic painter and lithographer Théodore Géricault. The painting depicts the French naval ship Méduse as it arrived in Mauritania on July 5, 1816 after experiencing problems on its journey leading to get damage to the Meduse as well as large numbers of casualties in the crew. The Raft of the Medusa was rife with homoeroticism and death. French critics at the time thought the painting was too gruesome and macabre. It wasn't gruesome and macabre to Dennis Nilsen though. He thought it was entrancing and wonderful. Nilsen said that looking at dead people made him feel invulnerable.

Despite the sullen picture Nilsen painted himself as a child, he was said to be a bit of a joker at school. The same was later said of Jeffrey Dahmer. Although he liked to think himself as highly intelligent and artistic, Dennis Nilsen was an unremarkable pupil at school. He didn't strike anyone as being especially bright. Nilsen was fond of history and art at school the most out of all the subjects. He hated sport and always tried to avoid taking part in any games. Dennis Nilsen joined the Army Cadet Force when he was fourteen. The Army Cadet Force (ACF) is a national youth organisation sponsored by the United Kingdom's Ministry of Defence and the British Army.

Dennis Nilsen grew up watching war pictures like The Dam Busters and had always liked the idea of joining the army one day. The main appeal of joining the army for Nilsen was that it would be a way to escape from Fraserburgh and the dreaded fish canning factory. Nilsen left school when he was sixteen. His first job was (no surprise here) in the fish canning factory in 1961. He knew he wouldn't be able to stomach this job for long. He found it tedious. Nilsen didn't want to be another of those local kids who left school, worked in the factory, and became trapped in Fraserburgh. He wanted to see something of the world.

People are, without even necessarily being aware of this fact, often a jumble of contradictions. Dennis Nilsen was, in his own mind, a rebel, radical, and non-conformist. He was a lone wolf who was suspicious of authority. And yet, he was also patriotic, old-fashioned, and loved cosy black and white war films. Joining the British Army seemed like a strange career choice for someone with such a strange sense of himself as Dennis Nilsen but maybe it wasn't that strange after all.

Nilsen was the ultimate outsider. No one is an outsider in the army. Having outsiders in the army would defeat the whole point of an army. More than anything, the dislocated young Dennis Nilsen simply wanted to feel like he was a part of something. The army therefore must have made perfect sense to him at the time. At the very least, it sounded a lot more appealing the fish canning factory.

* A surprisingly high number of serial killers received head injuries from an accident when still a child. There is a theory that this impairs the part of the brain responsible for ruminating on the consequences of one's actions. There seem to be no accounts of Dennis Nilsen suffering a bad head injury as a child. When he was later a teenage army recruit though, Nilsen allegedly had a scooter accident which resulted in a knock on the head. This head injury doesn't seem to have been very serious though or left Nilsen with any lasting medical damage that might explain the bizarre and disturbing nature of his later exploits.

THE ARMY GAME

Dennis Nilsen did his army training at St Omer Barracks in Aldershot. When he was a teenage army recruit, Nilsen also went on camping trips to the New Forest and Stonehenge. As an army recruit he also spent three Summer Camps at Fort Tregantal in Cornwall. He loved the West Country and described these years as the happiest of his life. Nilsen was very fond of cider when he was a young soldier and this obviously came as a consequence of being stationed in the West Country. It was in the army where Dennis Nilsen picked up his copious drinking habits.

Dennis Nilsen was never what you would describe as an alcoholic (Nilsen was always able to get up in the morning and go to work - he was always able to function in the way that a normal person would) but he did become a big drinker. He was happiest in a pub and always had alcohol in his flats. Many of his Nilsen's murders took place during a night of heavy drinking. Alcohol and music were the two crutches that Nilsen later used more than anything to escape from reality. He would crank up something on his stereo, put his headphones on, and then get blindingly drunk on rum, Bacardi, or whatever he had to hand.

When he was an army recruit, Dennis Nilsen would often wear a black cape when he went out at the weekend. The other recruits found this rather strange (not to mention pretentious). It felt like Nilsen was trying to assert some sort of individuality within the rigid conventionality of a uniform institution like the armed forces. The weekends were obviously the only time he could do this. The radical streak in Nilsen was never completely eradicated by the army. During his time in the armed forces, Nilsen once went to a Vietnam War protest in London and filmed it on his movie camera.

Some of those who served with Nilsen in the army were naturally later asked (in light of his infamy) what they remembered about him. The range of memories were mixed. Some remembered him as being a bully, others as a meek coward. Some said he was a goody two shoes and others said he was a rebel. Dennis Nilsen was all things to all people. Those that knew Nilsen in the army all tended to say though that he had quite bad personal hygiene and could be quite shy.

Eric Talbot, who knew Dennis Nilsen when they were teenage recruits, said years later - "We were both members of the same squad. He was a quiet chap, bit sheepish … he kept himself to himself really. He wasn't a great mixer. He didn't get stuck into sports like most of us did, I never saw him playing football, hockey, or getting involved with boxing. He had a weird sense of humour – totally different to everyone else's sense of humour. We couldn't work him out. He was also a bit of a bully in some ways, when he was a junior room corporal, he used to have a cane and he would smack people around their backsides … he would do it with juniors, but would never try it with lads in his own squad, they would have hit him back."

A former army sergeant of Dennis Nilsen was so astonished to later learn he was a serial killer that he tried to write to Nilsen in prison in the 1980s. What he hoped to accomplish by this is open to question. Maybe he just wanted to know what had gone so wrong in the life of the ordinary young man he used to know. Eric Talbot was naturally also astonished to see news of Dennis Nilsen's arrest in 1983. "When you sleep five beds away from somebody in a barrack room, it's hard to look at them and comprehend they are capable of killing all those people. People sometimes say, he must have been terrible. I say actually he was the most nondescript person you would ever meet. Nothing stood out about him as remarkable, he wouldn't shout his mouth off, in many ways he was the mouse in the corner."

Many of those that knew Nilsen in the army remembered him as being quiet and introverted. Nilsen was one of those people who blend into the background. Eric Talbot said that when he was in the army with Dennis Nilsen, the recruits went to Madam Tussauds and Nilsen was very entranced and fascinated by the chamber of horrors. When he visited Madame Tussauds as an army recruit, Nilsen even viewed the replica bath of John Haigh. * This is all rather darkly ironic because Dennis Nilsen's own bath would later end up in a macabre museum of the bizarre and he would also have his own waxwork in the Madam Tussauds chamber of horrors.

When he was an army recruit, Nilsen had to pass a course in map-planning. His ability to read maps was never much use to him in civilian life because he never had a car - a fact which was very fortunate because Dennis Nilsen could potentially have killed many more people if he had a car in which to transport remains and body parts! Dennis Nilsen passed Maths and English in his military exams. A former army colleague of Dennis Nilsen once described him as a pretentious pseudo-intellectual. Nilsen's precise IQ is unknown because he refused to take a test. We don't really know how intelligent he really was.

Nilsen did a lot of cross-country running when he was a teenage army recruit. He was always a lean and fairly fit looking man but he wasn't actually fit at all. He drank and smoked and later suffered from various medical ailments in the 1970s. Dennis Nilsen, who was brought up catholic, was apparently very religious when he was a young army recruit. Those who were in the army with Nilsen said that he was very prudish and disliked swear words and talking about sex. Religion was not something though that stayed with him in his life after the army. Dennis Nilsen was definitely not someone you'd find in church on a Sunday morning. He didn't even celebrate Christmas.

Nilsen said he always hid his sexuality when he was in the army - though there was no doubt in his own mind now that he was gay. Nilsen did encounter a few gay soldiers in the army but it was obviously something they were not very open or candid about. When Dennis Nilsen joined the army, homosexuality was still a military offence. It was still a civilian offence until 1967. Nilsen said he had his first gay sexual encounter in Aden when he was in the army. Nilsen is believed to have gone to Aden in 1967.

Dennis Nilsen said that when he was in the army he took advantage (sexually) of a couple of men who had passed out from drinking. One of these incidents took place on a train. Nilsen said that in the army he always avoided taking a shower with other men in case they deduced that he was gay. Dennis Nilsen said that he had sex with a female prostitute in Berlin when he was in the army but found the experience depressing. It merely confirmed to him that he was gay. When he went with the female prostitute in Germany, Nilsen boasted about the encounter to hide his sexuality but in reality he had found it a horrible experience.

Nilsen was stationed in Aldershot, Norway, Germany, Plymouth, the Shetland Islands, and the Middle East during his army career. Nilsen served in the British Army Catering Corps and was a chef in 1st Battalion the Royal Fusiliers. Nilsen always dreamed of doing something artistic for a living. Cooking in the army was the closest he ever got to this. It was in the army that Dennis Nilsen learned how to butcher meat. He would use this skill on his dead victims when he became a serial killer.

Dennis Nilsen was said to make a great curry and be an expert at whipping up omlettes. When he was in the army, he once cooked for the detainees at Al Masousa gaol in Aden - which was ironic in light of his later life. Dennis Nilsen was selected to cook for the Queen's Royal Guard in 1971. This never happened though because he was posted elsewhere.

Nilsen's regiment took part though in a parade in front of the Queen and Field Marshal Montgomery. Dennis Nilsen's mother said that when he visited home during his time in the army he was always proud to display his new cooking skills. Nilsen's visits home would become increasingly rare in the end though.

It is said that when he was stationed in Germany, Nilsen wanted to go and see Rudolf Hess in prison. The chances of a young army cook getting a meeting with Hess were pretty slim you would imagine! In 1970, Dennis Nilsen spent some time at an alpine ski resort in Bavaria with his army unit. During his time in Germany, Nilsen met a fellow soldier named Leslie Grantham - who was in the same regiment. Grantham would later become an actor and play 'Dirty' Den Watts in Eastenders. Nilsen said of Grantham - "I found him a good looking kid but he was a bit too aggressively extrovert in personality for there to have been any social rapport."

When Nilsen was posted to a Signals Squadron in the Shetland Islands, it is said that he used to enjoy taking part in Scottish country-dancing. You can't really imagine Dennis Nilsen happily country dancing but it did happen. On the Shetland Islands, Nilsen fell in love with an eighteen year-old private he met. The pair were friends and made some home movies on the islands. However, the teenage private in question was not gay and so did not have any romantic or sexual interest in Nilsen. Dennis Nilsen was so devastated that he burned all the home movies they had shot.

Dennis Nilsen said that when he was in Aden (now part of Yemen) the situation was volatile and getting out of control. The only thing the obstreperous factions there could agree on is that they should all target the British Army. Dead bodies were not new to Nilsen before he became a serial killer. He saw dead bodies in Aden. When he was in Aden, Nilsen was once nearly killed by a taxi driver who beat him unconscious and stuck him in the boot of a car. Dennis Nilsen managed to turn the tables on the taxi driver who attacked him in Aden. He ended up locking the taxi driver in the boot of the car. When he returned from Aden, Dennis Nilsen served with the Argyll and Sutherland Highlanders. They were stationed in Plymouth.

Dennis Nilsen served eleven years in the army and reached the rank of corporal. Nilsen said that one of the reasons why he left the army was that he was tired of moving around and living out of a suitcase. He had set his heart on living in London. Dennis Nilsen also suggested that one of the reasons he left the army was that he disagreed with the political situation in Northern Ireland and the army presence there. A former army colleague of Dennis Nilsen though refuted Nilsen's claim that he left the army because his political views were at odds with the presence of the British Army in Northern Ireland. This man said that Nilsen was a liar and that the real reason Nilsen left the army was because he got into a fight with a colleague. There is enough evidence to say that Nilsen got into more than one fight in the army. He could be a volatile character.

Dennis Nilsen was never terribly consistent when it came to why he really left the army. There were a range of theories put forward. The most credible theory is that Nilsen left the army in the end because of his sexuality. As he got older, he increasingly started to stand out like a sore thumb as an unmarried soldier. In those days it was obviously a lot more difficult to be gay in the armed forces. Nilsen also said that casual homophobia in the army made him want to leave. He was tired of having to hide who he really was. If that was really the case then his next career move was almost as strange as joining the army. In many ways it was actually stranger.

* John Haigh was a British serial killer known as The Acid Bath Murderer. He killed at least six people but (as ever with serial killers) the real body count might be higher. Haigh was basically a thief and conman who became inspired by the tale of Georges-Alexandre Sarret, a French killer who used sulphuric acid to dispose of victims. Haigh simply deduced that if he killed the people he had robbed and conned and dissolved their bodies in acid then no one would ever be able to finger him for any crimes.

In his younger years, Haigh worked as a chauffeur but pretended to be a solicitor. He was a very urbane sort of character who was able to deceive people (who should have known better) and win their trust. He was involved in dealing bogus stock shares and a compulsive thief. He is believed to have spent some time in prison during these years. Haigh, upon release, ruminated on his life and came to a rather disturbing conclusion. He decided that the reason why his career in crime had not taken off in the fashion he wanted was that the people he had swindled had been able to report him to the police. Why not simply kill the people he swindled? That way there would be no one to report his crimes.

Inspired by macabre tales of the French killer Georges-Alexandre Sarret, Haigh set upon what he felt was a surefire way to cover his tracks and dispose of his victims.

To test his dark theory, Haigh murdered a man and seized the man's bank savings and pension. He even sold the victim's house. The victim was William McSwan - a former employer of Haigh. Haigh was jealous of McSwan's luxury lifestyle and this was the motivation for the murder. He murdered McSwan by clubbing him over the head and dissolved the body in a vat of acid. When the parents of William McSwan became suspicious of their son's disappearance and asked Haigh about his whereabouts he killed them too in similar fashion.

Haigh was said to have run up large gambling debts around this time and, needing more money to fund his lifestyle, he decided to kill again. His targets this time were Dr Archibald Henderson and his wife Rose. Haigh stole a revolver from Henderson and used it to shoot both of them dead. Haigh then dissolved them in acid and sold all of their possessions. He did though keep their dog and car for himself.

There were six verified victims of Haigh in all but he is believed to have killed as many as nine people. He would move around a lot and often stay in hotels. When money became tight again he would simply look for some new wealthy victims to kill so that he could ransack their property and bank accounts. Haigh was very crafty and would often forge legal documents from his victims handing over their houses and finances to him.

John George Haigh was undone because of his past convictions for theft and fraud. When the police decided to investigate him in relation to some recent crimes they found that Haigh now lived in rooms with no drain access. Haigh had dissolved his latest victim in acid but then covered it in rubble (rather than dispose of it down the drain). The rubble was rather suspicious and the police investigated and thus revealed the dark secret of John Haigh.

The police proved there was human fat and remains in the rubble and - as a consequence - Haigh was sentenced to death and hung in 1949. The police actually found part of a foot in the rubble. Before he was hung, Haigh confessed to a number of murders which could never be verified because there was (obviously, given his strategy of dissolving victims in acid) no actual evidence or remains. His other victims are alleged to include two women. Haigh, urbane to the end, asked for a large brandy before his execution. He was a very calculating and ruthless man who only seemed to be interested in money. If he had to kill someone to get his hands on money it didn't bother him in the least.

WILLESDEN GREEN

In 1972, Dennis Nilsen moved to London to join the police. He is said to have briefly worked at a gay pub in Camden around this time too. Nilsen's sexuality is the obvious reason why he was drawn to London in the end. Although homosexuality was far less accepted in the 1960s and 1970s than it is today, it was obviously easier to be a gay man in London in the 1960s and 1970s than it would have been in a more remote part of the country.

There was still a strange contradiction in Nilsen's life in that he considered himself to be a very individual and anti-authority sort of figure and yet he joined the army AND the police - two bastions of conformity and tradition. Dennis Nilsen's desperate desire to belong and fit in somewhere seems the obvious explanation for why he joined the army and police - despite considering himself to be a rebel and radical. If it was no picnic being secretly gay in the army though, Nilsen found this state of affairs was even more difficult in the police.

It feels strange that Nilsen, after his time in the Army Catering Corps, never considered a career as a chef or in the food industry. Maybe he was bored of cooking after eleven years in the army? Those that knew Dennis Nilsen say that he seemed to have no interest in cooking whatsoever. He never cooked at home and never discussed food or recipes. After all those years in the Army Catering Corps, it felt like Dennis Nilsen never wanted to see another cooker again in his life. He probably would have been dismayed to learn that a cooker would still play a big part in his future - though certainly not for reasons that he might have suspected at the time.

Dennis Nilsen was a vaguely sinister looking man as an adult. He was one of those people who never seems to be smiling in photographs. Nilsen had bad eyesight and wore huge glasses. Nilsen had pale blue eyes and his glasses were clear-lensed aviators. It is a strange coincidence that so many famous serial killers seem to wear spectacles. Dennis Nilsen was 6'1 tall. He looks remarkably like the horror author Stephen King in some of his old photographs.

After he completed his police training course and passed his exams, Nilsen was posted to Willesden Green Police Station. Willesden is an area in north west London which forms part of the London Borough of Brent. It is situated 5 miles (8 km) northwest of Charing Cross. It is historically a parish in the county of Middlesex that was incorporated as the Municipal Borough of Willesden in 1933, and has formed part of the London Borough of Brent in Greater London since 1965. Nilsen found it fairly easy to get into the police because of his excellent army record. Dennis Nilsen was number Q287 when he was in the police. It is unavoidably weird now to see old photographs of Dennis Nilsen in a police officer's uniform. He seemed eager to make a career of this at first but his early enthusiasm didn't last.

Although he made some arrests while he was in the police, Nilsen never had to physically restrain or tackle a criminal. Dennis Nilsen sometimes walked the beat at Willesden Green on his own. If you lived in that area at the time you might well have walked past PC Nilsen in the street. Nilsen made several appearances in court in relation to arrests he had made. It is said that when Nilsen was in the police he was so enthusiastic to make a good impression that he even made a couple of arrests when he was off duty.

When he moved to London in the early 1970s, Dennis Nilsen would write to his mother now and again but contact with his family soon almost come to an end. It is possible that if Nilsen went home more often and actually liked his family (he genuinely didn't seem to like his relatives much at all) then his dark obsessions and desires might have been manageable or held at bay. One of the reasons why Dennis Nilsen hated going home was that his mother was always asking him when he was going to get married. He simply wanted to avoid talking about things like this. Dennis Nilsen's mother said he never once discussed his homosexuality with her. It was a subject he was deeply uncomfortable with.

After his arrest in 1983, the police found many letters in Dennis Nilsen's flat from his mother. He had never opened or read any of them. Nilsen's mother said she largely lost contact with him at some point after he left Scotland to join the army. Dennis Nilsen's half-brother Andrew would sometimes visit him in London in the 1970s but these visits were brief and few and far between. The psychiatrists who worked with Dennis Nilsen at his trial believe that his mental health (which was never exactly on rock solid ground to begin with) slowly began to erode when he cut off contact with his family. This left Nilsen feeling isolated and alone in the world. If he did miss his family though it was not something he ever confessed to.

Dennis Nilsen made some friends during his time in the army. He formed some connections. However, these connections were not permanent. They were fleeting. In his civilian life, Nilsen had no army colleagues that he maintained contact with. Nilsen was always puzzled by his inability to form lasting friendships. It was intensely painful for him to think that no one cared about him enough or enjoyed his company sufficiently to want to stay in contact over the long term. This was one of his motivations for moving to London. He wanted to find friends and maybe even lovers. He wanted to feel less alone in the world. More than anything Dennis Nilsen yearned for permanent companionship. He would eventually resort to desperate and extreme measures to achieve this.

The weird (weird in hindsight of his later crimes) thing about Dennis Nilsen is that he actually made quite a good police officer. Nilsen was a very pedantic, stubborn, and dogged sort of man. These were qualities that did him no harm in the police. After his time in the army (including war zones), Nilsen was also a fairly unflappable sort of character. He wasn't someone who was easily scared or easily thrown into a panic. The ability to stay calm in a crisis is something that all police officers have to learn but Nilsen already had this attribute.

However, despite his apparent aptitude for the job, his police colleagues never warmed to Nilsen at all. While army colleagues seemed to have conflicting views on Nilsen, the consensus of police officers was even less generous.

The police officers who served with Nilsen seemed to sense there was something dark about him. In the book House of Horrors by John Lisners, it is alleged that a former police colleague of Nilsen, on hearing later about the grisly story of murder unfolding at Cranley Gardens in the early 1980s, said - "If it's an ex-copper my money is on Dennis Nilsen." Nilsen found it relatively easy to adapt to army life and (later) working in a Jobcentre. The police force was more complex for him. It wasn't the day to day job that Nilsen found difficult but other police officers. Nilsen was an outsider in the police in a way that he wasn't in the army. Nilsen said that when he joined the police he was disappointed to find that the camaraderie he experienced in the army was not in evidence. His sexuality (though of course hidden as best he could) was plainly a factor in this.

It is naturally speculated that the main reason why Nilsen left the police was that such an occupation (in the early 1970s) made his gay lifestyle impossible. When he was a police officer, Nilsen once kissed a male friend while wearing his uniform simply for the thrill of it. He was near a train station at the time. Nilsen also once, while on patrol, discovered two men having sex in a car at night. He couldn't bring himself to arrest them or say anything and so just left them alone.

Incidents like this made Nilsen realise that it would be very difficult for a gay man like himself to be a police officer. Dennis Nilsen was not fey or effeminate though. It wasn't impossible for him to disguise his sexuality to most (if not quite all) work colleagues. All the same, he still felt an uneasy tension between his true nature and the profession he was now in. Nilsen later said that when he was in the police he couldn't see much difference between police officers and criminals.

When he was in the police, Nilsen lived in the Section House with other unmarried police officers. Nilsen once took a young man back to the Section House and had sex with him. The next morning, the sergeant was very suspicious when he saw the young man talking with Nilsen. The quick thinking Nilsen told his sergeant that the young man had just popped in because he was selling him a fish tank. This ruse just about worked. Dennis Nilsen hid his sexuality while he was in the police but some of his colleagues clearly had their suspicions. Nilsen said he left the police in the end because he wanted to have some fun. He realised pretty soon that this was the wrong career for him.

When he moved to London, Dennis Nilsen used the anonymity that a large city afforded to his advantage. He began to visit gay pubs and nightspots and meet transient and 'lost' young men. Dennis Nilsen said it was nerve-wracking to go in a gay pub in London for the first time. This was all new to him. In 1972, Dennis Nilsen joined the Campaign for Homosexual Equality. Nilsen began to drink more heavily when he moved to London. He used to visit a lot of pubs in Earls Court. These drinking binges made it difficult (but clearly not impossible) to hold down a job. Nilsen was desperate to find a lover and soulmate.

Nilsen never found his romantic ideal because his lovers irritated him in the end. He irritated them too. Dennis Nilsen was not an easy man to live with. He was quite bad tempered and became quickly irritated by petty things. You could suggest that he had inherited some of these traits from his mother. The men that lived with Nilsen often reported that they found him quite boring. Nilsen never went to nightclubs and had no interest in holidays. Nilsen's idea of a good night was watching an old film on television with a drink. His lovers and friends were always younger than him and he wasn't exactly the most exciting person to be with from their perspective.

Dennis Nilsen said he often found his drunken night jaunts

through the pubs and greasy spoon underbelly of London depressing but he was drawn out by a desperate longing for companionship. Although he was gay and promiscuous at a time when being gay wasn't nearly as accepted as it is today, Dennis Nilsen never went looking for sex in toilets or parks. He didn't approve of this behaviour. Dennis Nilsen said he did not have penetrative sex until he was 27. Dennis Nilsen loathed the casual nature of his relationships. He always yearned for a permanent companion.

Because of the police connection, Nilsen was later compared to John Christie. Christie was a killer who made 10 Rillington Place a notorious address in criminal history. Like Nilsen, Christie was an introverted man who killed his victims (his victims were women though and not men) in a grotty flat and then sexually abused the bodies. Like Nilsen, Christie also used to be in the police. It is alleged that John Christie's service as a Reserve Police Constable during World War 2 made the authorities initially reluctant to suspect him of murder.

John Christie, like Dennis Nilsen, tried to plead diminished responsibility due to insanity but the doctors deemed him sane. John Christie murdered at least eight people in London in the 1940s and 1950s by use of gas. Once they were unconscious he would rape and murder the victims. Like Nilsen, Christie seemed fond of necrophilia. Other serial killers who served in the police like Dennis Nilsen include Tore Hedin, Steven Calkins, Gerard John Schaefer, and the 'Golden State Killer' Joseph James DeAngelo.

Dennis Nilsen had to view some autopsied bodies in the morgue as a police officer. He found this experience completely fascinating and sexually exciting. Nilsen said that he once found the body of a dead teenage girl in the morgue attractive and exciting because she looked like a little boy. It is sometimes reported that Nilsen was booted out of the police for sexual indecency in the morgue. There is no evidence for this claim though. When he was a police officer, Nilsen and other recruits had to visit the morgue very soon into their service to get them used to dead bodies. Nilsen, as we have noted, was in his element but one recruit he went with actually fainted at the sight of autopsied bodies.

Dennis Nilsen lasted eight months in the Met Police before he quit and decided that this wasn't the career for him. Nilsen had to sell his general service medal after he left the police because he had so little money. He didn't have the faintest idea what he was going to do next. For the first time in his life he had no sense of direction. He only thing he knew for sure was that he wanted to stay in London.

MELROSE AVENUE

After he left the police, Nilsen dyed his black hair blond for a short period. He seemed to enjoy the sense of freedom he now felt after resigning from the Met. There was however the small matter of money. Nilsen was pretty broke and needed to find some work. In 1974, Dennis Nilsen worked as a security guard for a short time. He was a lodger at a house off Cricklewood Broadway during this period. When he lodged in the house off Cricklewood Broadway, Nilsen said other tenants would complain if he brought a man home. This cemented his sense of being an outcast in society just because he was gay. Nilsen used to drink in the Cricklewood Arms around this time. Years later the uncle of the DJ Fatboy Slim was the landlord.

When he was briefly a security guard, Nilsen's duties basically involved visiting various properties and buildings and having a look around to make sure everything was ok and that no one had broken in. Nilsen said that one night on his security guard duties he tried to have sex with a stuffed gorilla in the Natural History Museum. He found the sight of anything inanimate (even a stuffed gorilla!) strangely arousing. He didn't stick at the security guard lark for very long. After his time in the army and police it felt like something of a comedown to Nilsen to be a security guard. He knew he didn't want to do this long term. For a few months at the start of 1974, Dennis Nilsen worked in a cafe in Covent Garden but this didn't last long either.

In 1975 Dennis Nilsen was questioned by the police when a teenager named David Painter claimed that Nilsen had molested him and taken photographs of him while he was asleep without any consent. No charges were brought against Nilsen for the incident. When David Painter accused Dennis Nilsen of sexual assault, Nilsen was brought in for questioning at Willesden Green - the police station where he used to work. These were the first inlkings of the danger that Dennis Nilsen might potentially pose to others. Nilsen was always desperate to get young men back to his home. David Painter was perhaps the first of these young men to deduce that Dennis Nilsen was deeply weird and not a man that you should trust.

Nilsen eventually became a civil servant after he dropped out of the police. He was a recruitment interviewer helping the unemployed. When he inquired about a job at the local Jobcentre, Nilsen was practically hired on the spot because of his police and army record. Nilsen's specific duty at the Jobcentre was to help unskilled workers find employment. Nilsen took his position at the Jobcentre very seriously because he always liked to think of himself as a great champion of the underdog.

Nilsen was the Acting Executive Officer at the employment office on Denmark Street in Soho. Denmark Street was known as Tin-Pan Alley. A number of famous musical artists (like The Sex Pistols and David Bowie) recorded songs here. No one at the Jobcentres where Nilsen worked ever noticed anything especially dark or out of the ordinary about him. The ability of serial killers like Dennis Nilsen to appear normal to work colleagues has been described as the 'mask of sanity'.

What made Dennis Nilsen so disturbing in hindsight was the way he came across as completely calm and articulate in person. If you met him you would probably have no idea that he was so dangerous. Dennis Nilsen's other place of work was the Jobcentre in Kentish Town (where he was later posted in 1982). Nilsen's attendance record at the Jobcentres was said to be spotty at times. He compensated though by doing a lot of overtime.

Iain Mackinnon was later Dennis Nilsen's manager at the Jobcentre in 1980. In 2020, Mackinnon wrote - 'Des worked with me at the Jobcentre in 1980 and he was unquestionably odd. My wife recalled him saying in the office one day: 'You know it would be really easy to pick up some rootless young man in a bar and knock them off. Who'd notice? Who'd care?' Were the warning signs there? I'm not convinced they were. Des never gave me the creeps; I never felt uncomfortable in his presence. There is no doubt that he was a pain in the neck. He was confrontational and provocative in his opinions and eager to challenge authority. It could be said, though, that his willingness to over-share clashed with his reluctance to talk about himself.

'In the time I spent working with him, I never socialised with him. I did visit his ground-floor flat in Muswell Hill once, but not as a friend. He'd been off for a week with-out contact; there were no mobile phones then, and he lived alone. I was a conscientious young manager and lived not far away, so I popped round to see if he was OK. He was surprised that his manager might be genuinely interested in his welfare, reassured me that he was fine and would be back in on Monday. We chatted briefly and I left.

'Twelve people lost their lives in that flat. When I left, he gave me a farewell card he had made himself, wishing me well. It was a photo of the creation of Adam from Michelangelo's Sistine Chapel ceiling. Laid alongside it was a picture of Concorde. It baffled me and still does. What did it mean? After his arrest and before he was named, the papers simply said that the man arrested was a civil servant, a Scot, and a former soldier. I thought to myself: 'I know someone who fits that description. Could it be Des?' I decided it could be.'

Iain Mackinnon said that he didn't like Nilsen to deal directly with the public at the Jobcentre and this greatly irritated Dennis Nilsen. 'I once informed Des that I would not allow him to work with the public: 'Your manner in relationships with your colleagues is usually outspoken and often overbearing. I am concerned that... your manner with the public might cause offence,' I wrote to him. His reaction was furious; he threatened to sue me for libel, though he backed down in the end, as he usually did.'

Dennis Nilsen actually got a promotion when he worked at the Jobcentre. Though argumentative, he was considered to be good at his job. Staff at the Jobcentre where Nilsen worked said he had a habit of telling the same corny jokes all the time. Those that knew Dennis Nilsen said he had what you might describe as a very dry and dark sense of humour. Nilsen worked as a civil servant for nearly a decade. It was clearly a job that he liked and was happy to stay with. He found that the staff were a broader mix of people than he'd encountered in the police force so this made it easier to blend in and not stand out. Nilsen said that the women in the Jobcentres where he worked all knew he was gay. It was a female sixth sense. No one cared that Nilsen was gay. It was a much more liberal and relaxed atmosphere than the Met Police.

The staff at the Jobcentres where Nilsen worked were never invited to any of his flats. He never forged any close friendships with work colleagues. Dennis Nilsen would occasionally go for a drink with work colleagues but he never stayed for long. He would always make his excuses and go off alone to a gay pub. Dennis Nilsen used to drink in The Coleherne in Earls Court. Gay celebrities like Freddie Mercury, Kenny Everett, Anthony Perkins, Rupert Everett *, Ian McKellen and Derek Jarman were seen in this pub. In 2008, it was rebranded as a gastropub - The Pembroke. Colin Ireland, a later killer who targeted gay men, used to go in some of the same pubs that Nilsen previously used to frequent.

Those that went to the pub with Dennis Nilsen say that he was always sullen and quiet at first but then, when he became drunk, would get more and more talkative to the point where no one else could barely get a word in. Dennis Nilsen was especially fond of The Golden Lion pub in Soho. In the late 1970s, this was one of only two pubs in the whole of Soho listed in the Gay News. Given his love of pubs at night and habit of drinking at home until he passed out, it is remarkable that Nilsen was ever able to get up and go to work. His time in the army obviously must have left him with a body clock that always woke him at the crack of dawn.

Dennis Nilsen was a union representative for the civil service. Nilsen was said to be a very demanding union rep. He helped to organise the picket of Garners steak houses in 1979. Nilsen was famously pedantic and dogged in his duties as a union rep. He could usually be relied on to make any dispute worse rather than better. Nilsen would leave London now and again to attend trade union conferences around the country. This was later tragic for his third victim Martyn Duffey because they met at Euston Station when Nilsen was on the way home from a conference.

When the police searched Nilsen's flat after his arrest they found a badge from the 1981 People's March for Jobs. Despite his interest in politics, Dennis Nilsen never actually joined a political party though. In 1983, he wrote a letter to the Guardian from prison complaining they had wrongly written that he was a member of the SDP. Nilsen liked to think of himself as an independent radical socialist. He never found any political party he wanted to join. People who knew Dennis Nilsen before he was arrested say that his biggest pet peeve was Margaret Thatcher. Any mention of Thatcher would activate a long and bitter rant from Nilsen.

In 1975, Dennis Nilsen began a relationship with a man named David Gallichan. The first address that Nilsen and David Gallichan shared was a bedsit on Cricklewood's Teignmouth Road. David Gallichan (who had moved to London from Somerset) was a homeless man that Nilsen met in a pub. Nilsen intervened when Gallichan was being accosted by two men.

David Gallichan was known as Twinkle. It was Nilsen who came up with this nickname. Nilsen always liked to come up with nicknames for his friends and lovers. David Gallichan once told a newspaper that Nilsen was terrible in bed and never had much interest in sex. Gallichan later denied though that his relationship with Dennis Nilsen was a gay relationship. This latter claim doesn't seem very credible.

Dennis Nilsen's estranged biological father passed away in the 1970s and left Nilsen £1000 (which would be ten times that in today's money). Nilsen used the money to move into a ground floor flat at 195 Melrose Avenue, Willesden Green. Nilsen and Gallichan moved in together at Melrose Avenue and were happy at first. Nilsen and David Gallichan spent many hours gardening together. Nilsen even planted some plum trees when he lived at Melrose Avenue though he wasn't there long enough though to see any fruit. The arrangement where Nilsen had the garden at Melrose Avenue to himself was something he worked out with the estate agents. At the time of this arrangement he obviously didn't know that he would end up needing the garden to dispose of dead bodies.

Dennis Nilsen never really had any enduring friends. His acquaintances were people who drifted in and out of his life. They were casual lovers or people who just needed a roof over their head for a few weeks. David Gallichan was the closest he came to a lasting connection but even this relationship was not permanent. Nilsen's casual friends and lovers were always much younger than him. This is part of the reason he could never form a meaningful connection. They never shared his interests or tastes in music and films. Dennis Nilsen said that when his relationship with David Gallichan was starting to collapse he brought a Swiss woman back to the flat in an attempt to prove to himself that he was bisexual. This experiment was a predictable failure.

It has been speculated (though never proven) that one of the reasons why David Gallichan and Dennis Nilsen fell out is because Gallichan did not share the necrophilic fantasies of Nilsen. Old home movies of Dennis Nilsen and David Gallichan together strongly suggest that Nilsen was the dominant personality in the relationship. One can see in them that Nilsen is an irritable man who likes to be in control of a situation - however trivial the situation is. Nilsen always seems to be in a bad mood in these amateur films. Nilsen had a smart appearance in the police and army but by now his hair was more out of control and he appeared more frazzled and wild eyed. You could say that he was starting to look slightly more like a serial killer.

The reason why David Gallichan said he left Dennis Nilsen is that he found their relationship to be increasingly constrictive. David Gallichan didn't like just being with one person as if he was in a conventional marriage. Nilsen claimed though that he ordered Gallichan to leave. Whatever the truth, the fact that Nilsen was left all alone was devastating for his already fragile mental health. When Gallichan eventually decided to leave, this left Nilsen feeling lonely and abandoned.

David Gallichan said that six months after he moved out of the flat at Melrose Avenue, he met up with Nilsen for a drink. Gallichan said that he felt rather hurt though when Nilsen declined an offer to take the details of where Gallichan was living now. The fact that David Gallichan eventually moved out of Nilsen's flat could be seen as a lucky escape. It doesn't seem impossible that Nilsen might have killed Gallichan in the end. Dennis Nilsen murdered someone for the first time only eighteen months after David Gallichan moved out of the flat they shared.

After David Gallichan moved out, Dennis Nilsen had a relationship with a man named Steven Martin. Martin left Nilsen for another man - this rejection merely compounding the sense of alienation and frustration that Nilsen felt. David Gallichan later passed away in 1992. He was interviewed by the police after Nilsen was arrested and said that Dennis Nilsen had never tried to harm him during their relationship. Rejection by David Gallichan may have been a salient catalyst in Dennis Nilsen becoming a killer. Nilsen never wanted anyone to leave him again - even if it meant he had to kill them in order to prevent this from happening.

* In a 2021 interview, the actor Rupert Everett said of Nilsen - "He was in the pub that I used to go to. Yeah, so I could be dead. He used to go the Coleherne, which was this leather bar. I didn't know him but he was there. I mean, that's where he got two or three of his victims from." Everett said it was entirely possible that he might even have met some of Nilsen's

future victims in the pub and spoken to them.

LOVE OF THE DEAD

Dennis Nilsen's killing spree took place from 1978 to 1983. Nilsen's passion for necrophilia * was the main motive for his murders. By the time he reached his late twenties, Nilsen was aware that he found dead people more attractive than living ones. The literal translation of necrophilia is 'love of the dead'. Necrophilia is a pathological fascination with dead bodies which takes the form of a desire to engage with them in sexual activities. Serial killers aside from Nilsen who indulged in necrophilia include Ted Bundy, John Christie, Gary Ridgeway, Ed Gein, Edmund Kemper, and Patrick Kearney. Necrophilia is a common postmortem activity for sexual serial killers because it doesn't give the victim the opportunity reject the offender. Dennis Nilsen said that when he killed someone he was especially excited by the loose limbs 'dangling' when he picked up the body.

Dennis Nilsen said that he experienced an excited feeling of power at the control he had over dead bodies. It is a common thread with many serial killers that their sexual fantasies from a young age are about people who are restrained, can't move, or are dead. Studies have shown that necrophilic serial killers are much more likely to mutilate and cut up the victims. Dennis Nilsen confessed that he did sexually abuse the dead bodies of his victims but said it was non-penetrative. Reflecting on the murder of his first victim, Dennis Nilsen wrote - 'It was the beginning of the end of my life as I had known it. I had started down the avenue of death and possession of a new kind of flat-mate.'

Dennis Nilsen embraced his 'career' as a serial killer quite late in life in comparison to many killers. A large number of serial killers kill for the first time in their teens or twenties. According to the Crime Classification Manual, a serial murder is defined as 'three or more separate events in three or more separate locations with an emotional cooling off period in between homicides'. This classification is very flawed though because, according to its strict criteria, Dennis Nilsen is not a serial killer! Typically, a serial killer's 'cooling off' period between murders will involve them going back to their 'normal' life for a time. The FBI generally states that one must kill three people to qualify as a serial killer. There must also be a gap between each killing (a bomber, for example, is a mass murderer or terrorist as opposed to a serial killer).

Dennis Nilsen is difficult to explain because, as we have noted, he didn't have some of the common factors we associate with the development of serial killers. He didn't even take drugs. Dennis Nilsen said that he never had any interest in hard drugs and that alcohol was his main vice. Nilsen was definitely odd and isolated but many people are eccentric or alienated and would never harm a fly. The fact that Dennis Nilsen was a potential monster was something that didn't seem blindingly apparent or obvious to those that knew him. There was palpably a darkness to Nilsen but no one could have dreamed of how dark he really was at his core. A lot of serial killers have a superficial charm which lulls victims into a vulnerable state. Nilsen never displayed much evidence of having any charm but most of his victims clearly trusted him and didn't seem him as a threat.

Dennis Nilsen's victims were usually (but not always) gay men of no fixed abode. Gay male serial killers always seem to prey on the same sex - just as heterosexual male serial killers will usually target women. Financial gain or theft was never a motive in Dennis Nilsen's murders. None of his victims had any money. Nilsen is said to have torn up the money he found on one victim. A number of Nilsen's victims were young men or teenagers who were homeless or had nowhere to stay that night. It is common for serial killers to target homeless people because not only are these victims vulnerable they are also less likely to be reported missing. A shameful thing about the Dennis Nilsen case is that the conditions for a situation like this to arise again still exist. There are still marginal and forgotten people in society whose disappearance would hardly be noticed.

Dennis Nilsen would sometimes trawl through Piccadilly Circus looking for men to talk to and take home. He even later used to go to video game arcades looking for young men. He must have cut an unlikely figure, shuffling through an arcade as Pac-Man and Space Invaders beeped away in the background. None of Nilsen's verified victims were over the age of 27. Dennis Nilsen's first victim was Stephen Holmes. Stephen went missing in December 1978 on the way home from a pop concert and was only fourteen years-old. Stephen Holmes spent the night with Dennis Nilsen but Nilsen didn't want Stephen Holmes to leave and so strangled and drowned him. He washed the body (including the hair) and later abused the corpse sexually after initially storing it under the floorboards. Jeffrey Dahmer said he killed his victims so that they would never be able to leave him. This is exactly what Dennis Nilsen said too.

Dennis Nilsen claimed he thought that Stephen Holmes was 17 and didn't know he was 14. This could be true or it could have been a case of Nilsen not wanting to admit that he had picked up and killed someone who was still more or less a child. If Nilsen's autobiographical notes are anything to go by, the sexual fantasies he shares suggest that he might have targeted children in the end. Nilsen said that because people had seen him leave a pub with Stephen Holmes, he had expected the police to knock on his door that week with questions about a missing boy. However, to the surprise of Nilsen, they never did. It came as a genuine surprise to him how easy it was to kill someone and apparently get away with it.

A number of Nilsen's victims were very short and small. This was probably no coincidence. Nilsen obviously wasn't going to try and kill someone who might overpower him. The fact that Stephen Holmes was a victim was only verified when Nilsen identified a photograph of Stephen years later in 2006. Although it was established in 2006 that Nilsen had murdered Stephen Holmes, he was never charged with this murder because it was not deemed to be in the public interest. One of the deciding factors was obviously the fact that Nilsen was already serving a life sentence without any possibility of parole anyway.

After he killed for the first time, Nilsen purchased an electric knife to dismember the victim but couldn't go through with it. He then began to see the beauty (from his point of view) in a dead body and decided to wash and keep the corpse. Nilsen said that when Stephen Holmes was under the floorboards his curiosity got the better of him and he simply had to take a look. This would become a regular feature of Nilsen's murders. The corpse would become like a possession or toy for Nilsen. He would derive a bizarre sense of comfort from having a dead body to talk to or sit with.

Dennis Nilsen said that at one point he hung the body of Stephen Holmes by the ankles so that his fingertips were grazing the carpet. Dennis Nilsen's behaviour with the bodies of his victims was truly bizarre. He would treat them as if they were still alive and they were his new housemate or boyfriend. Many serial killers keep trophies or keepsakes from their crimes. It is speculated that for Nilsen, keeping the dead bodies served as his form of trophies.

When he first tried to put a victim's body under the floorboards, Dennis Nilsen found it impossible because rigor mortis had set in. He had to manipulate the limbs to make the body more flexible. Ted Bundy and Gary Ridgway would leave the bodies of their victims in the woods and go back and have sex with them until such time as decomposition made this impossible. We see similar behaviour in Dennis Nilsen - although his victims were always in his flats. Experts believe that most serial killers have a 'comfort zone' in that they tend to 'hunt' in places they are familiar with. This was certainly the case with Dennis Nilsen. He killed men he had met in local pubs.

Nilsen's other verified victims were Kenneth Ockenden, a 23 year-old Canadian tourist - who Nilsen strangled with his music headphones in 1979. Sisteen year-old runaway Martin Duffey, who Nilsen killed in May 1980. Twenty-six year-old William Sutherland, was killed by Nilsen in August 1980. Nilsen said he woke up to find Sutherland dead in his flat and had no memory of how or why he killed him. Sutherland was a male prostitute that Nilsen met near Piccadilly Circus. Malcolm Barlow was a 23 year-old epileptic orphan who Nilsen killed in September 1981.

In 1982, Nilsen murdered 23 year-old John Howlett and 27 year-old Graham Allen. Nilsen's last verified victim was 20 year-old Stephen Sinclair at the start of 1983. There were other victims that Nilsen claimed to have murdered but could not remember the names of. These other victims remain unidentified. It is believed that nine victims were killed at Melrose Avenue. The last three victims died at Nilsen's last flat in Muswell Hill. The families of Ken Ockendon and Billy Sutherland both reported their disappearance.

Nilsen was later dubbed The Muswell Hill Killer by the British press. Dennis Nilsen was convicted of killing six men. He claimed to have killed fifteen when he was arrested. He later retracted this and said the actual number was twelve. In his prison 'memoir' though, Nilsen claimed to have killed two more men who were never reported missing.

The fact that Nilsen never revealed all the names and details of his victims is open to interpretation. It is entirely possible that he genuinely couldn't remember all the details because he was somewhat drunk during many of these murders. However, it is equally true that serial killers often hold onto secrets because this is the only way they can retain some sense of power and control once they have been caught. Dennis Nilsen said that he would suffer blackouts when he drank too much. This was the explanation he gave to police for why he couldn't remember all the names and details of several of his victims.

In 2020, a former soldier named Bob Cowan said he had an encounter with Dennis Nilsen at King's Cross Station in 1978 when he was twenty years-old. "This man sidled up to me on the station concourse," recalled Cowan. "He was tall, slim and wore glasses. He told me his name was Des. I must have stood out like a sore thumb. I was short, looked young, had blond hair and blue eyes, and was clutching my Army suitcase. He told me he was an ex-soldier and asked me if I wanted to come for a drink. He bought me a beer and asked if I wanted a game of cards. We played but he was letting me win, I could tell. He was plying me with drink.

"He suggested that we go back to his flat to keep drinking and playing. I got the feeling he wasn't all he seemed. But I just thought he was some sad, lonely man. He told me he had been with a Scots regiment and was a cook. It's something that always stuck in my mind. He kept trying to convince me to come back to his. I just thought, 'No way'. I had a girlfriend and a train to catch. I made my excuses and left. I'm so glad I didn't go with him that day. I thank God I had my wits about me. It was one hell of a close shave."

One wonders how many others had a close escape from the prowling Dennis Nilsen. Quite a few it seems.

Also in 2020, a man named Nick Barritt said he got chatting to Nilsen at Waterloo Station in 1979 when he was 24 years-old and was invited back to Nilsen's flat. Barritt, to his eternal relief, declined the offer. Barritt said that Nilsen got 'stroppy' when the invitation was declined. Barritt must have been incredibly relieved at his decision to get away from Nilsen when he saw the awful news in 1983 about a serial killer in Muswell Hill with a flat full of body parts.

"I was in a bit of a pickle and he sort of came out of nowhere," said Barritt. "He told me he'd missed a train too - although he later admitted he hadn't - and said: 'I'll buy you supper'. I had 36p in my pocket and very little other options so I decided to go with him. I went along and we walked to the Strand Cafe where we both ordered beef burgers, chips, peas and carrots. I remember him speaking in a soft Scottish accent. He kept staring at me and didn't say much. He seemed a bit agitated. He kept getting a cigarette out to light and then putting it back - hesitating.

"After dinner he invited me back to his flat in Muswell Hill to stay on his sofa. He was insistent, saying he'd pay for a taxi back to the flat and then would pay for me to get a cab to the station in the morning - but I was worried I wouldn't make my early train on time. As soon as I went to go he got quite stroppy about it - bordering aggressive. He told me 'that's no reason, I bought you dinner. I expect you to come back, it's not going to cost you anything'. He told me he had all the booze - whisky and the like - that I could want. But I thanked him, shook his hand and started walking back to Waterloo. Now I dread to think what might have happened if I'd gone with him."

A man named Paul Dermody lived with Nilsen for two weeks at the end of 1978. Dermody later said that Nilsen was an insufferably pompous and overbearing man who was impossible to live with. In 1979, Nilsen put a tie around the neck of a Chinese student named Andrew Ho as part of a 'bondage game' and tried to strangle him. Ho, fortunately, managed to kick out at Nilsen and run out of the flat. There was no doubt that Nilsen had tried to kill him. Ho went to the police but, shamefully, they did not investigate the incident or even talk to Nilsen.

Dennis Nilsen said he was attracted to Asian men and targeted a couple of students from the Far East like Ho. Dennis Nilsen said he was never attracted to muscular men. Nilsen said that he never found hairy men attractive either. Nilsen's 'type' when it came to men often seemed to be people who were short and fair-haired. Dennis Nilsen's romantic ideal was someone much younger than him. Nilsen always seemed to want to be a dominant mentor figure to his lovers.

Dr David Holmes said that "Dennis Nilsen was a serial killer who was a wonderful chameleon. He disappeared into society, he didn't stand out. He was probably someone who would make others probably feel at ease, usually the destitute. In the case of Nilsen, he enjoyed people that were very passive. He didn't want interaction much. He enjoyed the company of someone who was pronate, didn't do anything. Who he could kind of feel strong and powerful with." Dennis Nilsen himself said - "My offenses arose from a feeling of inadequacy, not potency. I never had any power in my life."

There was a gap of one year between Nilsen's first and second murder. Dennis Nilsen's second victim was the Candadian tourist Kenneth Ockendon in December 1979. Dennis Nilsen met Kenneth Ockendon in the Princess Louise pub in Holborn. The pair went on a sightseeing tour of London and drank together for several hours. When they went back to the flat, Nilsen learned that Ockendon was going home to Canada the next day. Nilsen couldn't bear the thought of Ockendon leaving so he killed him and kept the corpse for company. Dennis Nilsen said he used to put the dead body of Kenneth Ockendon to bed and say 'good night' to him.

Nilsen admitted that he would talk to the corpses of his victims as if they were alive. Dennis Nilsen also liked to sleep next to the bodies of his victims. Nilsen said he would put underwear, socks, and a vest on the bodies of his victims when he 'brought' them out to watch television with. Nilsen's victims were all young. They tended to see him as a kindly father figure - which was obviously a tragic mistake on their part. Nilsen later watched Shaw Taylor on Police Five (a Crimewatch style TV show of the era) appeal for any news people might have about the missing Kenneth Ockenden.

In 2016, Radford University produced a report which stated that 21% of serial killer victims are killed by strangulation. This was how Nilsen killed his victims. He never used firearms or knives. Dennis Nilsen often used a ligature to strangle his victims. Often it was a necktie. Nilsen said he never had sex with any of his victims when they came back to his flat. Those who managed to escape from Nilsen all reported that there had been some form of (non-penetrative) sexual contact though. Dennis Nilsen would burn evidence of his victims on a bonfire when he had access to a garden. However, this never alerted any suspicion in the area. One could hardly blame the neighbours. If you see someone having a bonfire the last thing you assume is that they are burning the dead body of someone they have just murdered!

Nilsen had to throw some tyres onto the bonfire to mask the odour of burning flesh and organs. Dennis Nilsen said he would sometimes vomit in the garden at Melrose Avenue when he was burning the bodies. When he had bonfires at Melrose Avenue, Nilsen always had to tell curious children attracted by the bonfire to keep back in case they might see any human remains or bones. Nilsen used lighter fuel to make sure he got a good blaze going. After one of his bonfires, Nilsen said he had to crush a skull with a rake. The bonfires that Nilsen had at Melrose Avenue would burn for hours long into the night.

Dennis Nilsen became skilled at dissecting a human body. This is a grisly but unavoidable task for serial killers who murder at home. Dennis Nilsen chopped up some of his victims and stuffed them in the floorboards of his flat at Melrose Avenue. One can only imagine how that place must have smelled. There were a few incidents of neighbours complaining of a smell coming from Nilsen's 195 Melrose Avenue flat but Nilsen told them that the odour stemmed from structural problems in the building.

Nilsen stored some of the remains of victims at Melrose Avenue in suitcases which were sometimes put in the shed. Nilsen said that storing remains in the shed at Melrose Avenue attracted a lot of flies but it wasn't too risky because the smell from the garden was not unlike compost. Because he didn't drive, disposing of remains and bodies was a constant struggle for Dennis Nilsen. Nilsen once dropped a carrier bag of human remains in the street by accident when he was walking his dog. The remains were found by a member of the public and reported but nothing came of this.

When he lived at 195 Melrose Avenue, Dennis Nilsen was once
a victim of burglars and two detectives came to the flat. When
Nilsen was burgled and two police officers came to the flat, at
one point they were standing directly above the remains of two
victims under the floorboards. Nilsen was amazed that the
detectives didn't notice the foul odour seeped into his home
from all the body parts. Nilsen was equally amazed that they
didn't notice anything suspicious about him. According to the
book Dark Secrets of the Black Museum, Nilsen once let a
room at his flat in Melrose Avenue fill with smoke while three
guests were sleeping in there. It was apparently a genuine
attempt to suffocate them.

Nilsen would sometimes bury body parts underneath bushes.
He would also slip some human remains between two fences
for them to be eaten by garden animals. When Nilsen was
arrested and the story of his murders broke, a Daily Mirror
reporter rushed down to Nilsen's old home at Melrose Avenue
because he'd heard that the police were going to search and dig
up the garden there. The reporter spoke to a dog walker who
told him that his dog had uncovered some very strange bones
in the park that was close to Dennis Nilsen's old garden.
Nilsen obviously disposed of some remains in this park.

Nilsen said he scattered the internal organs of his victims in
different places. When he chopped up the bodies of his
victims, Dennis Nilsen had to strip to his underwear to avoid
getting stains on his clothes. He was very skilled with knives
because of his years as an army cook. Nilsen sometimes put
the torsos of victims in suitcases until he had a chance to burn
them. Near Melrose Avenue, a man is alleged to have once
found a ripped plastic bag that seemed to contain a rib-cage.
The man did not report this though - presumably because it
hadn't occurred to him that the bones might be human.

Dennis Nilsen's old two-bedroom flat at 195 Melrose Avenue is
still there. It has of course been completely refurbished and is
valued at around £500,000. This first flat where Nilsen killed

people could not be knocked down because it was part of a street of connected houses. Many people who have lived in the house in recent decades say they were either not bothered by the fact that Dennis Nilsen once lived there or had never heard of him. When he lived at 195 Melrose Avenue, Dennis Nilsen blocked off the side entrance to the garden so that only he and David Gallichan could use it.

In the late 1970s, a ten year-old boy in Cricklewood said that Dennis Nilsen had indecently assaulted him. No charges were brought in the end because the boy's parents did not want to put him through the ordeal of a police investigation and possible court case. By the late 1970s, Nilsen was completely out of control. His life had become a strange and disturbing nightmare. Jeffrey Dahmer said he tried to use religion to stop himself from killing but it didn't work. It's hard to know what Dennis Nilsen could have turned to in an attempt to quash his own equally grim and deadly desires. He'd lost contact with his family and had no permanent companion save for alcohol and his dog.

In 1979, the Jobcentre had a big Christmas party that Dennis Nilsen helped to organise. Nilsen brought in some pots and pans and cooked for eighty people. It is of course rather harrowing to think of what those pots and pans might have been used for in Nilsen's flat. Nilsen cooked in the army 'galley' style and gave his cooking skills a rare display. Dennis Nilsen also liked to make mulled wine for his work colleagues at Christmas. Late in 1978, Dennis Nilsen had written that he felt crushed and forlorn by his 'treadmill' of work, drink, and isolation. By the end of the decade he had slipped down the rabbit hole of madness. But how long would it take for the outside world to actually notice?

* Dennis Nilsen would bathe the bodies of his victims in the bath after he had killed them. Nilsen said he enjoyed caring for the corpses of his victims and liked to dress them up. As we have seen, Dennis Nilsen would sometimes position the body

of a victim next to him and watch television with them. Necrophilia was something that he was clearly obsessed with from a young age. When he killed, the only motivation of Dennis Nilsen was to have a dead body as a plaything. This clouded any compassion or logic.

'Necrophilia, which is frequently taken to mean a sexual attraction to corpses, is defined by the DSM-V as "an other specified paraphilic disorder, involving recurrent and intense sexual interest in corpses",' wrote psychologytoday. 'However, since necrophilia was first documented in Krafft-Ebing's Psychopathia Sexualis, there has been a lot of variation discovered in those who engage in this behavior, and subsequently many attempts to produce a cohesive classification. Necrophilia is not associated with any one mental illness or disorder. However, it is known that some necrophiles had previously been diagnosed with Conduct Disorder and Antisocial Personality Disorder [4]. Necrophiles with this diagnostic history have increased likelihood to commit homicide before carrying out necrophilic acts, simply because diminished empathy and antisocial behaviour are characteristic of these disorders. There has also been suggestion that those who have committed necrophilia have suffered from depression and schizophrenia in the form of anthropophagy and vampirism.

'Many researchers and authors have posited their ideas behind necrophilic motivation, and one of the primary reasons given is the need for an unresisting or unrejecting partner. This reason is worth unpacking, as on the surface it seems to indicate a violent offender asserting his will over his victim and abolishing their will completely. This is no doubt true of those who commit sexual homicide, but what about necrophiles who find other ways to come into contact with a corpse? The need for an unrejecting partner is universal for most humans who desire an intimate relationship with another living human, as is the need to feel accepted.

'And so with necrophilia, it would be worth assessing all of the qualities people look for in a living person (using dating websites, and the ample pop psychology outlets), and seeing if those needs could be met with a deceased partner. A dead partner is not judgmental, there is no fear of needing to produce a reciprocal orgasm during sex, they cannot emotionally hurt anyone, they can be trusted, they do not answer back, there is no concern about offspring, and they can meet what is only a temporary need for sexual intimacy. The necrophiliac also has the luxury of creating, imagining, or fantasizing the corpse to be anything they want it to be. (It is worth noting that a sex doll also fulfils these needs, and it is perhaps a worthwhile study to explore a history of sex doll use in the lives of necrophiliacs.)

'Necrophilia will never be neatly defined. We can only do our best to classify, but at the same time understand the limitations and usefulness of our classifications when assessing necrophilic case studies. To understand the motivations of the wide array of necrophiles, we need to understand the motivations of loving the living, and see under which contexts a person's preferences might change to focus on the dead. We must also consider the barriers to necrophilia such as smell (addressed here), and how a person is able to "give themselves" permission to become intimate with the dead; for example, we see in those with Antisocial Personality Disorder, or a history of Conduct Disorder, that a conscience is lacking. Once we can start putting these building blocks together, law enforcement can become better informed, and greater strides can be made in knowing the risk factors that lead one to necrophilia.'

CRANLEY GARDENS

Serial killers tend to broadly fall into two categories - organised and disorganised. Organised serial killers are the ones who maintain a job and might even have a wife and children. Disorganised serial killers are completely detached from society. One might argue that Dennis Nilsen fell somewhat in the middle of these categories in that he held down a job but was dangerously alienated from society in his private life. Nilsen was capable of going to work in the morning and coming home and walking his dog. He would make small talk with people in the local off-licence and tell corny jokes to work colleagues. Nilsen was able to function at a certain basic level.

Once he went home though and shut the door, Nilsen's life was a paranoid nightmare. He would put his headphones on and listen to music for hours on end as he got more and more drunk. There were times when Nilsen felt as if his music headphones were the only thing that stopped him from falling into oblivion. Music was the only means of escape he had from the nightmare he had created for himself.

Nilsen always looked lean and fit but this was misleading. He had smoked since he was fourteen and was a heavy drinker. Dennis Nilsen's favourite rum was Captain Morgan's Black Label. Dennis Nilsen and Jeffrey Dahmer both had the same favourite tipple. They were both partial to rum & coke. Dennis Nilsen was also said to drink a lot of Bacardi and Coke. Those who visited Dennis Nilsen say that he was quite fond of whiskey too. Nilsen drank lager now and again but he preferred spirits. Nilsen liked to get drunk as fast as possible. Nilsen was relying on alcohol more and more now in his private life. Residents at Cranley Gardens when Nilsen lived there said that whenever they bumped into Dennis Nilsen they could usually smell alcohol on his breath.

Despite his fabled army cooking skills, those who visited

Dennis Nilsen said that he very rarely had any food in the cupboard or his fridge. David Gallichan said that Nilsen never cooked and got by on cheap takeaways. Despite his time as a cook, Nilsen was a man of simple tastes when it came to food. He liked takeaways, fried eggs, and crisps - which obviously wasn't what you would call health food. Those that knew Dennis Nilsen said it was hard to believe he was a trained chef because he hardly ever used his oven. Nilsen didn't care if he had to get by on a piece of toast for his dinner. He seemed to have little interest in food. It appears as if eleven years in the Army Catering Corps had put Nilsen off cooking for life. He simply couldn't be bothered with it. You probably won't be surprised to hear that there are no instances of Nilsen ever hosting a dinner party.

Dennis Nilsen had an operation for gallstones in 1975. Nilsen said that he also picked up some STDs in the mid 1970s. He had a dose of gonorrhoea and crabs. Dennis Nilsen had a bout of scabies too in the 1970s. His physical health was poor and his poor diet and heavy drinking only made it worse. Nilsen was a mental and physical wreck by the end of the 1970s but he was able to hold it all together somehow and give the impression of a man who was still in control. His years in the army had taught him to repress any outward signs of emotion or discomfort.

In 1980, a young man named Douglas Stewart woke up to find Nilsen attempting to throttle him. He managed to escape and reported what had happened to the police. However, the police, as in the similar incident with Andrew Ho, took no action over his claims. It is speculated that because homophobia was rife in the police at the time they simply dismissed the incident as a 'homosexual lover's tiff' that was not important enough to divert any resources to. It is an awful reflection on society and the Met Police that in the early 1980s a serial killer was at large targeting the gay community in North London and yet no one even seemed to notice.

Despite his sexuality, Nilsen once brought a young woman

back to his flat for a drink. He did not harm her though and only killed men. Nilsen would have derived no sexual satisfaction from having the corpse of a woman. Dennis Nilsen had to leave 195 Melrose Avenue in the end because the landlord wanted to renovate the flat and get rid of him. The agents of the flat were so desperate to get Dennis Nilsen out of Melrose Avenue that they offered him £1000 to leave. They also said they knew of a flat in Muswel Hill where he could move in.

Nilsen, being the type of stubborn character that he was, would ordinarily have been expected to dig his heels in and refuse to move out but the money was too good to turn down. His position at the Jobcentre was not exactly a high salary job so pragmatism dictated that Nilsen should swallow his pride and take the £1000 (which would be three times that amount in today's money). It was a tidy sum. Nilsen must have been worried about the remains he'd left in the garden and house but he managed to burn everything before he moved out. If the flat at Melrose Avenue was going to be gutted and renovated that was surely good for Nilsen because it would destroy any lingering forensic evidence.

Dennis Nilsen was very good at saving money. Aside from alcohol, he didn't really spend money on anything. Dennis Nilsen said that material things held no interest for him. He once said that he never dreamed of winning the football pools. Dennis Nilsen clearly had no interest in fashion. He often wore the same shirt and was conservative in style. He never seemed to collect or buy anything and didn't have a car. He didn't go to fancy restaurants. He didn't go to the cinema. He never went on holiday. His money simply went on rent and booze.

Dennis Nilsen's last home at Flat 23D Cranley Gardens, Muswell Hill. He moved here in 1981. Cranley Gardens was about four miles away from Melrose Avenue. Muswell Hill is a suburban district of north London. It is mainly in the London Borough of Haringey with a small part in the London Borough of Barnet. Even when Dennis Nilsen lived there, Muswell Hill was a middle-class sort of area with families and nice houses. The house that Nilsen lived in was pretty tatty by the standards of most residents in the area. The house at Cranley Gardens had been divided up into a number of flats. Nilsen was not someone who needed much space to live in. At both Melrose Avenue and Cranley Gardens he slept in the same room that served as the living-room.

The cooker in Nilsen's Cranly Gardens flat was already there when he moved in. He never cleaned it so it was pretty disgusting. Nilsen only ever used the hob rings. Nilsen's attic flat at Cranley Gardens was very cramped. All the ceilings were sloped. The crime scene photographs of this flat after Nilsen's arrest show it be a claustrophobic and squalid place. It's hard to believe anyone was even allowed to rent it out as it was. Most people would have refused to live in the flat as it was. They would have wanted it decorated and painted and given new furnishings at the very least.

The landlady at Cranley Gardens when Nilsen was there lived in India. Apart from collect the rent she evidently never did much with the house. There were a high turnover of tenants and the house was left to decay. Nilsen's flat at Cranley Gardens had a rusted grease encrusted gas-cooker and an old water heater. It was freezing cold in the winter and the paint on the wall was flaking. Tiles on the roof were missing. This was a grim place to live. There were five other tenants at Cranley Gardens but because Nilsen kept himself to himself none of them ever talked to him much. You had to go up three small flights of stairs to get Nilsen's pokey attic flat at Cranley Gardens.

After his move to Cranley Gardens, Nilsen didn't commit any murders for nearly two months. There are instances of serial killers who have long gaps between murders. Nilsen was capable of not killing for months at a time but he was still prolific in a fairly short period. One shudders to think how many people he might have killed if he hadn't been caught. When he moved to Cranley Gardens, Nilsen no longer had access to a garden and so disposing of the bodies became much more difficult. Dennis Nilsen would boil down the flesh (specifically the heads, hands, and feet) of his victims in a large cooking pot. Nilsen would sometimes (though rarely) take drink or food into work for colleagues. This food was almost certainly cooked in the same pot that he used to boil the heads of his victims.

One of Dennis Nilsen's victims was a young man named Malcolm Barlow. Barlow suffered from epilepsy and had been found by Nilsen in the street looking unwell. Nilsen got him an ambulance and they parted. Tragically though, Barlow returned to Nilsen's building the next day and waited for him to get home from work. Barlow wanted to thank Nilsen and had obviously formed an attachment to Nilsen too. He probably considered Nilsen to be a nice and kind man. Nilsen found Barlow's presence an irritation and so he killed him.

After he had washed the bodies of his victims, Nilsen would often dress them in his own clothes. He said he would use washing-up liquid to wash the bodies. Jeffrey Dahmer would sometimes take a shower while there was a dead body stored on the floor of the shower. Nilsen did something similar - though he only had a bath. Nilsen said that he sometimes used to bathe in the same water that he had used to wash the bodies of his victims. Dennis Nilsen said that he would shave his victims as part of the process of 'caring' for their bodies. Nilsen's mental illness was illustrated by the lack of hygiene he exhibited.

Dennis Nilsen seemed to kill people who irritated him. Most people irritated Dennis Nilsen so few were safe if they went home with him. Nilsen was almost impossible to live with over a long term because he was so irritable and bad-tempered. Anyone who lived with him was bound to annoy him in the end and the feeling was mutual. Those who lived with Nilsen found him too constrictive and sullen a personality to put up with. If you lived with Nilsen you felt as if you were constantly walking on eggshells all the time. Nilsen must have known this himself. He knew he was doomed to end up alone. Only with a dead person did he feel content. Going to prison was really a step up for Nilsen's social life. At least he would never be alone again.

Dennis Nilsen's motive for murder was almost identical to Jeffrey Dahmer. They both, in their warped way, decided that being with a dead person was better than being alone. Dennis Nilsen said he felt a 'spiritual communion' with his victims. Dennis Nilsen had a Polaroid camera and used this to take photographs of victims. Dennis Nilsen once wrote - 'I think that in some cases I killed these men in order to create the best image of them. It was not really a bad but a perfect and peaceful state for them to be in.'

Dennis Nilsen, as was his custom, ate and slept in the same front room at Cranley Gardens. Martyn Hunter-Craig lived with Nilsen for a time at Cranley Gardens and said he genuinely had no idea that Nilsen was killing people. Martyn Hunter-Craig said that Nilsen was very passive and disinterested in bed and never gave the impression that he wanted a sexual relationship with a living person. It is occasionally speculated that Nilsen might have been influenced by the 1972 Alfred Hitchcock film Frenzy. Frenzy is about a London serial killer who strangles his victims with a necktie.

Martyn Hunter-Craig said that Nilsen was always watching cowboy films on television - which Hunter-Craig found boring himself. Nilsen's younger friends and lovers never shared any of his interests. Although he considered himself to be a film buff, those that knew Dennis Nilsen in London say that he never went to the cinema. Nilsen didn't like cinemas because you couldn't drink in them. Ted Bundy said he often got drunk before he abducted and murdered someone. This is a pattern we see with Dennis Nilsen too. Ted Bundy would sometimes put makeup on people he had murdered. Dennis Nilsen did the same thing. Nilsen liked to put makeup on his victims to hide the post-mortem discolouration.

Carol Stottor reported Dennis Nilsen to the police around this time after he was nearly suffocated and drowned by Nilsen (but then revived and allowed to leave - it is very rare for serial killers to do this) but the police only contacted Stotter again AFTER Nilsen was arrested. Paul Nobbs, another potential victim who survived a close encounter with Nilsen, said that he did not report his experience to the police because he knew they wouldn't do anything once they found out he was gay. Carol Stottor said that his encounter with Dennis Nilsen was so frightening and confusing that he was only able to fill in all of the blanks through flashbacks and nightmares.

'In April, 1982, Nilsen entertained a drag artist named Carl Stotter, 21,' wrote CrimeLibrary. They drank together and went to bed. He attempted to strangle Stotter, who woke up, unable to breathe. He thought Nilsen was trying to help him, but that was not the case. Nilsen carried him into the bathroom and placed him in a tub of water, submerging him several times until Stotter begged for him to stop. Stotter then went under and stopped struggling. Nilsen thought he was dead and carried him to the couch. Bleep (Dennis Nilsen's dog) jumped up and began to lick Stotter's face, aware that he was still alive.

'Nilsen then took him to bed and wrapped himself around the young man until he regained consciousness. Nilsen told Stotter that he had gotten his throat caught in the zipper of the sleeping bag that had covered him. Stotter attributed the experience to a bad nightmare, despite getting a check-up and learning that his condition was consistent with severe strangulation. He actually agreed to meet Nilsen again, but did not keep the appointment. He also did not go to the police.'

Carl Stotter later wrote to Dennis Nilsen to ask why he had attacked him. From prison, Nilsen replied - 'What passed between us was a thin strand of love and humanity'. Stotter had no idea what Nilsen meant by that and you can hardly blame him. In 2011, Carl Stotter complained about the news that Nilsen had received financial aid in prison. "Why should he have his human rights when his victims haven't any? It's not justice. This happened to be 29 years ago and I never forgot it. I feel really angry, but this is not just about me. It is about all the people he killed too."

Carl Stotter battled alcoholism after the Dennis Nilsen trial. He died in 2013 after falling into a diabetic coma. Carl Stotter's sister said in 2020 - "Carl was scared stiff of giving evidence and seeing Nilsen again. He was so confused about why he was still alive, and was haunted for the rest of his life by survivors' guilt. He didn't start drinking until about two years after the court case, but once the alcohol got him that was it. It was all downhill from there."

Dennis Nilsen, as we have noted, loved music and used it as a source of escape from reality. One sinister thing he would sometimes do with victims was put headphones on them and sneak up behind them while they were absorbed in the music. Dennis Nilsen was a fan of "O Superman" - a 1981 song by performance artist and musician Laurie Anderson. Carl Stotter said he listened to O'Superman when he was with Nilsen. This song sounds incredibly sinister today because it makes you think of Dennis Nilsen. Nilsen said that after one murder he slumped into a chair and listened to O'Superman eight times in a row.

Nilsen said that when he got drunk and listened to music through his headphones he would be transported away and experience flashbacks of his life and childhood. Those who escaped from Dennis Nilsen said that he always remained calm - even at the point where he tried to harm them. Carl Stotter said that Nilsen seemed completely trustworthy. No one seemed to sense the awful danger than Nilsen posed. Dennis Nilsen had a vague sort of plan in place for any (would be) victim who escaped and contacted the police. Nilsen was going to say a struggle ensued because they'd tried to rob him.

John Howlett (who was killed in 1982) is the Nilsen victim

who put up the biggest struggle. Dennis Nilsen said at one point Howlett even tried to strangle him until he managed to turn the tables. Nilsen strangled John Howlett with some loose upholstery on his armchair. However, Howlett survived this so Nilsen had to drown him in the sink. Dennis Nilsen said that there were a few times when someone knocked on his door while he was cutting up a body. Nilsen told the visitors it wasn't a good time and that they should come back later.

Jeffrey Dahmer world spray paint the skulls of his victims to use in a shrine. Nilsen never did anything like this. Dennis Nilsen always claimed that he couldn't stand the sight of blood. Although he said he couldn't stand the sight of blood, Nilsen clearly had a strong stomach. He was capable of cutting bodies in half, hacking off limbs, and boiling heads. The fact Nilsen strangled his victims supports his claim that he didn't like blood. Nilsen owned cooking knives but he never stabbed his victims. Nilsen is actually said to have got his cooking knives from one of his victims. Dennis Nilsen said that chopping up bodies was difficult and physically demanding. He would sometimes cut himself by accident with the knives while he was doing this. Nilsen used a chopping board to dissect parts of his victims.

Dennis Nilsen's murders are felt to have been spur of the moment because of his great difficulties in disposing of evidence. There wasn't much sign of any planning or thought about them. After he washed the bodies of his victims, Nilsen would put talcum powder on them. Dennis Nilsen specifically targeted passive victims. He wanted to feel dominant even before he killed them. Many of Dennis Nilsen's victims did not go back to his flat because they were sexually interested in him but because they needed somewhere to stay that night. Dennis Nilsen said that he would sometimes discover a dead body in his flat in the morning and have no memory of the murder that had obviously taken place.

Nilsen sprayed the rooms in his flats a couple of times of day to try and reduce the fly infestation. When he stuffed the remains of his victims under the floorboards, Dennis Nilsen inevitably developed a problem with flies and maggots. When he had a dead body under the floorboards, Nilsen would spray insecticide and deodorant down there twice a day.

It is speculated that Nilsen wasn't too bothered the awful smell of his flat at Cranley Gardens in the end because he had become used to it. Carl Stottor, one of the potential victims who managed to survive, said that Dennis Nilsen's flat did smell but he put this down to the fact that Nilsen had a dog. Carl Stotter said the Nilsen's flat was shabby and smelly but he'd been in worse before. The mind boggles at how terrible these 'worse' flats must have been.

Nilsen, inspired by John Haigh, said that he considered dissolving the remains of his victims in the bath but never went ahead with this because it was impracticable. He had no idea where to get hold of vast quantities of acid and knew it would be a highly suspicious thing to try and purchase or use. Despite his grisly activities there is no evidence that Dennis Nilsen was inspired by nor especially interested in any famous serial killers. Nilsen liked to think he was unique. He loathed being compared to anyone else.

After he boiled the head of a victim, Nilsen would pick off the flesh and put it down the toilet. The process of boiling flesh was very time consuming. Nilsen must have spent hours doing this. Dennis Nilsen would sometimes lose track of where he had left body parts and was surprised once to open a cupboard door and find a pair of severed legs inside.

This was why he tried to boil the flesh away. Dennis Nilsen left the eyes in when he boiled heads.

Nilsen said before he cut up a body he would go to the pub first and steel himself for the task by getting drunk. He would then, as we have noted, continue to drink when he got home. Dennis Nilsen was said to always have the windows of his flat at Cranley Gardens open. This does not come as a surprise. It would have been bizarre if he didn't. Dennis Nilsen would boil hands and feet for hours to separate the flesh from the bones. He would put the bones in the dustbin.

Nilsen would sometimes flush pieces of flesh that weighed two pounds down the toilet. It genuinely didn't seem to occur to Nilsen that he might be storing up trouble by putting flesh down the toilet. The possibility of a blocked drain was something that he didn't anticipate. Nilsen would sprinkle salt on the remains of victims to try and stave off the decomposition and the smell. Jeffrey Dahmer liked to keep bones and skulls belonging to his victims. This is not really something that Nilsen did. Once decomposition set in, Nilsen would then begin the grisly process of disposing of the evidence. Dennis Nilsen would often use a sliced open bin liner to put under bodies he cut up. Nilsen kept parts of his victims in a wardrobe and tea chest.

Nilsen said he would cut through torsos at the waist. He quickly learned what the quickest way to cut up a body was. Graham Allen was Nilsen's second to last victim. Nilsen kept Allen's body in his bath for several days after he killed him. Dennis Nilsen said he had to get drunk before he could face up to dissecting his victims. Nilsen would put plastic sheets or bin-liners on the floor before he dissected his victims. He said he would vomit in the sink a few times while he did this grisly task. Nilsen said that after he killed his last victim Stephen Sinclair, he washed the body and lay on the bed with it for a time. He then went to work.

Even in the midst of his gruesome squalor, Nilsen would leave for work each morning at 8am. It was remarkable really that, in the midst of his murders and grisly circumstances, Nilsen was able to maintain some semblance of a routine and go to work. He was on a sort of automatic pilot. Dennis Nilsen said he usually kept one 'fresh' corpse in a cupboard and would take it out when he wanted some company. Nilsen's ideal companion was someone who just listened and never talked.

Nilsen said that he once contemplated suicide but did not go through with it because his dog came in and licked his face. He didn't want to leave the dog all alone. According to the book Dark Secrets of the Black Museum, Dennis Nilsen did consider feeding parts of his victims to his dog (as a way to get rid of evidence). This was not something he actually did though. In 1983, The Guardian reported that Dennis Nilsen had once left a bag of human intestines at a bus stop. That may or may not be true but Nilsen was incredibly cold and callous in the way that he disposed of victims. This was a man with a lump of coal for a heart.

THE PLUMBER

Dennis Nilsen was captured because a plumbing company was called out to unblock the drain outside the house where he had his flat at Cranley Gardens. Nilsen was no genius when it came to covering his tracks and disposing of evidence. It was almost as if he wanted to get caught. Film and TV often depicts serial killers as elusive criminal masterminds who are always two steps ahead of the police. The reality is very different. Most serial killers are of average or below average intelligence and not exactly impossible to catch. Dennis Nilsen made such an obvious blunder that we can only presume that, even on a subconscious level, it was partly intentional.

As we have seen, Nilsen had been flushing body parts and bones down the toilet. The drain incident that led to Nilsen's capture began when one of the downstairs residents complained that his toilet wouldn't flush. When he learned that someone was having trouble flushing the toilet in the house at Cranley Gardens, Nilsen didn't realise at first that he had caused the blockage by flushing remains down the toilet. He was a bit slow on the uptake. When he first heard that there might be a problem with the drains, Nilsen stopped flushing his own toilet.

The bizarre thing about Nilsen's capture is that he himself wrote a letter to the landlord complaining about the drain being blocked! In his bizarre letter to the agents complaining about his toilet not flushing, Nilsen also complained about the flickering lights in the communal areas of the house. Given that he had been rumbled and was about to be arrested this was an eccentric letter indeed. We can only presume some sort of deflection was intended. Nilsen might have deduced that he would not be suspected of blocking the drains if it came to light that that he had written a letter of complaint about them.

Mike Cattran was the Dyno-Rod employee called out to unblock the drain. He said the smell of human decay when he lifted up the manhole cover was overwhelming. Nilsen went out to see what the fuss was all about and tried to suggest to Mike Cattran that the drains to his building must be blocked with fast food. This ruse obviously didn't work. After Dyno-Rod were called out to unblock the drain, Nilsen made an attempt to remove bones and flesh from the drain himself but it was too late. The flesh and bones that clogged the drains had attracted a lot of rats. Mike Cattran said that the drain outside Nilsen's building contained a foul smelling sludge and about thirty pieces of flesh.

When Mike Cattran examined the sludge blocking the drain at Cranley Gardens, he said - "I haven't been in this job for long but I know that isn't s***." Nilsen later sneaked out at midnight with a torch and carrier bag. He removed the flesh in the drain and slung it over a back garden. His actions merely made the situation look more suspicious. Nilsen said that his planned course of action with the blocked drains had been to buy some Kentucky Fried Chicken, remove the bones, soak it in water, and then put it down the drain. While he was confident that this plan would work, he did not go through with because he felt sure that he would probably kill someone again soon and then he would be right back to square one with no way to get rid of the escalating evidence. Nilsen seemed to decide at this point that he had had enough of this bizarre and ghastly nightmare he had created for himself.

Mike Cattran told the tabloids at the time - "I could tell it was full, so the blockage was between that and the manhole cover. There was a terrible stench when I lifted the manhole cover and climbed down 12ft to the bottom. When I got down there I couldn't believe it. I pulled out lumps of flesh the size of my fist and strips of flesh that looked as though they had been cut from an arm. I went down again with a plunger. As I pushed it down towards the mains, the whole lot moved and my bottle went. There was a bit with hair on it. The flesh was so white and there was such a lot of it. I was trying to think what sort of animal it could be. As I was prodding around, I thought it's obviously not a dog, there's no fur. It's not a chicken – not that much of it. It was all bruised up and eventually I got to thinking that it had to be a body."

Mike Cattran had to return the next day to confirm his grisly suspicions. "I was determined not to be proved wrong about what I had seen so I climbed down to look for more. I reached down the pipe and there was some more there −bits of what could be fingers and strips of flesh. I lined the fingers up with my own and thought they could be that bit from the palm to the first knuckle and other bits up the second joint. Then one of the girls who live there came out of in her dressing gown, white-faced with her hands shaking and offered to call the police." It's fairly obvious that Dennis Nilsen didn't know much about plumbing. He hadn't anticipated that he might end up blocking the drains with his habit of flushing victim remains down the toilet. Tests on the bones and remains blocking the drain later found that they were human and the drainpipe led directly to Nilsen's flat.

When word got out that human remains were blocking the drains at the flats in Cranley Gardens, the residents immediately thought that Nilsen was the prime suspect. He was far and away the strangest and most enigmatic of the people who lived in the building. When the police were called out about the blocked drain at Cranley Gardens, the residents told them that there was a 'peculiar' man who lived in the attic. Hywel Jones, one of the police officers who worked on the case, believes that deep down Dennis Nilsen wanted to be caught. "In my opinion Nilsen got bored of killing and wanted to be found for the fame, so he blocked his drains with the bodies instead of burying them."

It took about an hour for a pathologist to confirm that the flesh found in the drain at Cranley Gardens was human. As soon as the police took some of the flesh away as evidence the fate of Nilsen was sealed. Nilsen's trip outside at night to remove the evidence from the drain at Cranley Gardens was almost certainly doomed from the start. Nilsen, on a tentative first attempt to explore the drain at night, was spotted by one of the other residents and asked what he was doing. Nilsen said that he had come out for a pee but he didn't seem convincing. Two of Dennis Nilsen's neighbours later said they had heard the noise from Nilsen removing the manhole cover to the drain at night. One didn't need to be Sherlock Holmes to deduce that Nilsen's behaviour was all very suspicious.

The day that Dennis Nilsen was arrested, he went to work as usual. Nilsen said that he mentally prepared himself for his arrest while at work that day. He knew that the police were going to arrive soon in connection with the blocked drain. On his last day at work in the Jobcentre, Nilsen wore a scarf that had belonged to his last victim Stephen Sinclair. Nilsen said to work colleagues that he if he wasn't at work the next day it would be because he was either dead or in prison. They all thought he was joking and laughed.

Nilsen made no attempt to flee when he neared arrest. Nilsen said that the reason why he didn't flee was because he knew it was useless. He knew he wouldn't have got very far and had nowhere to go anyway. Dennis Nilsen later said that it would have been a cowardly act to try and flee and avoid arrest. Detective Chief Inspector Peter Jay said that when they told Dennis Nilsen they were investigating his drains, Nilsen smirked and said "Since when have the police been interested in blocked drains?"

When the police first went to see Nilsen, he pretended to be surprised and appalled at the news that human remains had been found in the drains. He quickly realised the game was up though and confessed to many murders. * People who lived in the street where Nilsen had his last flat were shocked and amazed that such horrific things were going on in such a mundane and ordinary place. Once he had accepted that the game was up, Nilsen told the officers who had come to his building - "It's a long story. I'll tell you everything. I want to get it off my chest."

When the police arrived it was almost a relief to Nilsen that this madness was nearly over. Dennis Nilsen had a Border Collie cross dog named Bleep. When he was arrested he was more worried about what would happen to his dog than what would happen to him. Dennis Nilsen clearly liked animals more than people. Nilsen said he briefly considered suicide when the man came out to unblock the drain and it dawned on him that he had caused the blockage. He obviously didn't go through with it though.

When the police first entered Flat 23D Cranley Gardens, they had to fight the urge to vomit. The smell of death and decay was awful. Detective Chief Inspector Peter Jay said that he immediately detected the scent of rotting flesh when he entered Nilsen's flat. When the police searched Nilsen's flat they encountered a nightmarish scene. Nilsen had body parts and torsos hidden all over the place. He even had bags containing the heads of some of his victims. The police found a scented candle in Nilsen's flat when he was arrested. The candle couldn't mitigate the awful smell of the place. DCI Jay said that when he entered Dennis Nilsen's flat it was damp because winter sleet was coming in through an open window. The smell of death and decay was still powerful though.

Detective Inspector Steve McCusker also experienced the dreadful smell when they first entered Nilsen's flat. "It was absolutely incredible, but unfortunately it was a smell we as police officers were aware of. As soon as we walked in, we knew a dead body was lying somewhere in that flat." DC Brian Lodge, who worked on the Nilsen case, said that when he went into Nilsen's flat - "I remember lifting the upturned drawer in the bathroom and seeing a pair of legs sticking out of a black bin liner." When he was arrested, Nilsen had a skull wrapped in a plastic bag inside his tea chest. The police found a number of body parts in Woolworth's carrier bags.

Although he later had a bookish reputation in prison, there wasn't much evidence of a book collection in Nilsen's flat when he was arrested. Dennis Nilsen's belongings didn't amount to much. Apart from cutlery, pots and pans, a small television, and a radio-cassette player, Nilsen hadn't really collected anything of note. When the police searched Nilsen's flat they found a number of cassette tapes. Nilsen was fond of The Stranglers - which was bleakly ironic to say the least. The music that Dennis Nilsen listened to was very dark. There wasn't much evidence (apart perhaps from Abba) of jaunty pop music in his collection.

Dennis Nilsen was a fan of Journey to the Centre of Frankenstein by The Edgar Winter Group. Nilsen was also a fan of the composer Mahler and the musical work Fanfare For The Common Man. Dennis Nilsen also liked The Who's rock opera Tommy, Mike Oldfield's Tubular Bells, the Russian composer Shostakovich, and the composer Aaron Copland. Dennis Nilsen said of his state of mind prior to killing his seventh (unidentified) victim - "I had drunk a considerable quantity of Bacardi, and the piece of music I was listening to finished – Incantations by Rick Wakeman – and I felt exhilarated. I was on some sort of high." Nilsen's possessions in his flat included (as you might expect) several air fresheners. Some joss-sticks were also found in Nilsen's flat when he was arrested. Jeffrey Dahmer also used incense to try and disguise the aroma of death.

Dennis Nilsen's last flat was in a very grotty and squalid condition when he was arrested. It was absolutely filthy with plates and empty food containers piled up. The oven was covered in dirt and grease and everything was old, tattered, rusted, and falling apart. The police found mothballs in one of the bags containing remains of Nilsen's victims. Mothballs are small balls of chemical pesticide and deodorant used when storing clothing and other articles susceptible to damage from mould. People with an interest in true crime are often confused at how killers like Jeffrey Dahmer and Dennis Nilsen lived in apartment buildings and yet no one noticed the smell! The only explanation for Nilsen is that he eventually lived in what was essentially an attic room.

Brian Lodge was the police officer in charge of the exhibits in the Dennis Nilsen case in 1983. Lodge said years later that he was amazed Nilsen wasn't caught sooner. "The first four or five bodies, he kept under the floorboards or under the kitchen sink in a cupboard – they must have been rotting. Why that smell was never noticed by neighbours, I'll never know." A police chief said that searching Jeffrey Dahmer's apartment was like entering some nightmarish museum of the macabre. The police officers who first entered Dennis Nilsen's flat had exactly the same experience. Nilsen had a few house plants in pots in the flat when he was arrested. They were literally the only nice things about the place.

Stephen Sinclair's lower torso and legs were found under Nilsen's bathtub. Twenty year-old Stephen Sinclair was the last victim and was killed in January 1983. Stephen was a heroin addict who Nilsen had bought a hamburger and then taken home. The police had to 're-assemble' Stephen Sinclair on a mortuary slab to identify him. After he was arrested, one of the many pieces that Nilsen scribbled in a writing pad was titled The Last Time I Saw Stephen Sinclair. This was a strange thing to write of someone he had killed. Nilsen even said he would have liked to have got to know Stephen Sinclair and said he wished he hadn't killed him.

Letters for Nilsen at Cranley Gardens were left on the ground floor to be collected and nearly always addressed to Des Nilsen. The other residents of the house therefore assumed that the attic tenant was named Desmond Nilsen. They had no idea his name was Dennis. The police believe that Nilsen's adoption of the name Des was almost like transforming himself into another character. Des was his affable alter-ego and plain old Dennis Nilsen was the killer.

After he was arrested, Dennis Nilsen's mother was besieged with reporters and journalists at her home in Scotland. She would speak to them but always refused to take any money whatsoever for talking about her now notorious son. Dennis Nilsen's mother was (understandably) perplexed when it came to light that her son was a serial killer. She said that the kind and gentle son she knew wasn't capable of such things. In his unpublished writings, Nilsen later seem to blame his mother for the way he had turned out. This seemed somewhat unfair to say the least.

While she stood by him, Dennis Nilsen's mother did at least accept he was guilty. There have been cases where the mothers of serial killers refuse to accept their son did anything wrong or would be capable of murder. Ted Bundy's mother always steadfastly insisted he was innocent right up to the point where he faced the electric chair and finally confessed. Dennis Nilsen claimed that he broke off contact with his mother by letter in 1985. When he was arrested, Dennis Nilsen's mother gave the tabloids photographs of him when he was younger because she 'wanted the son she knew' to appear in the papers. Dennis Nilsen's mother died in 2010.

Dennis Nilsen was driven to Hornsey police station after his arrest. Nilsen spent his nine months on remand at Brixton Prison. After Dennis Nilsen was arrested, the first thing the estate agents had to do before they put his flat on the market was completely renovate the kitchen and put new fittings in. Dennis Nilsen's flat was decorated and put back on the market at £60,000 (this was 1983). The tabloids (predictably) dubbed the flat the 'house of horrors' and wondered who on earth would want to live there. A surprisingly large number of people viewed the flat merely so they could gawp at the notorious place where all these grisly and awful things happened. When he heard that his flat at Cranley Gardens had been dubbed the House of Horrors by the press, Nilsen wrote in prison that the only House of Horrors he knew was 10 Downing Street.

* 'Once the killings began, it appears he became addicted to the feeling of power and control it gave him and so the behaviour progressed more and more. He is known to have killed at least 12 young men and possibly as many as 16 or more,' wrote Psychopaths in Life. 'He seemed completely

oblivious emotionally to the fact he had irreversibly taken the lives of a dozen or more young people. His confession is also somewhat unusual in that there was no denial or resistance.

'He just calmly admitted to the murders, as though he knew the game was up. There was also perhaps some kind of intellectual (not emotional) understanding that if he wasn't stopped he would just keep going. The matter of factness aspect of his character showed up in another way it often does in psychopaths, in that on one level he lived a perfectly normal life and appeared in one sense to blend into society. He held a job down as a civil servant and appeared on a certain level, on first impressions at least, to be quite normal.

'It is this aspect of a hidden life or identity which often shows up in psychopaths, whilst a respectable facade of mask of sanity is presented to the world, which covers the reality of the disorder and chaos that's really going on in their psyche. The nature-nurture argument will continue on but to most sensible explanation for many is still that both genetic and environment play a role. Serial murderers are probably not born to kill but are born with a disposition towards psychopathy that is later activated and brought out by a poor environment or some kind of deep trauma. Many of theses trauma and difficulties are avoidable with better parenting and nurturing and for this reason it can be argued that society must take some responsibility for the creation of psychopaths.

'How are we raising our children? How are we treating them? Unsympathetic and non empathetic parents do exist and a combination of this with already dormant psychopathic genetics may be what creates the Dennis Nilsens of the world. The hugely insensitive treatment by his mother regarding the death of his grandfather, the only person with whom he was very close, still remains an unanswered question, a pivotal turning point in his life and huge red flag regarding the quality of his upbringing.

'It may not therefore be fair to say Dennis Nilsen was "born to kill". He may have had a faulty gene which set him off in that direction but several avoidable events may have pushed him over the edge and sealed his fate. More research must be done to improve parenting to the point that these "psychopathic triggers" which enhance a pre-existing disposition are not unnecessarily pulled by insensitive and abusive behaviour. This view is further enhanced by the apparent trend of psychopathic traits increasing rather than decreasing in the population. This is an indication that there is something we are doing in society to increase these traits.'

THE SECRET GARDEN

When he examined one of the pieces of flesh found in the drain at Cranley Gardens, the police pathologist Professor David Bowen noticed a ligature mark. Hair analysis was used on the hair found in the drain at Cranley Gardens. The police actually had to use an anthropologist to try and make sense of the bones and remains found in the wake of Nilsen's arrest. The police also used a ballistics expert to verify Nilsen's confession that he had dissected the bodies with knives. A lot of cleaning products were found in Nilsen's flat when he was arrested. Not that they made much difference. The place still looked filthy. DCI Jay described Nilsen as 'extremely odd' to colleagues after they arrested him. Dennis Nilsen said that when he was taken to the police station he had a fear that the police might hang him in a cell and pretend it was suicide.

Detective Inspector Steve McCusker took the famous full length photograph of Dennis Nilsen after his arrest. It was not standard procedure to do this but McCusker said he knew that Nilsen was going to be national news. "There was just something else as well – it's hard to describe, within my mind that this case is going to be famous or infamous, whatever way you want to look at it. And I thought, I'm gonna take a picture as he is now, just in case anything happens. So I stood him up against the wall when we got him back to the police station and I took the camera from the charge room and just took a long, full-sized photograph of him. It was an unusual thing to do in those days – in fact it is very unusual to do it today."

Although he did not turn himself in, Dennis Nilsen was one of those serial killers who seemed relieved to have been captured. He was honest enough to admit that he would have killed many more times if given the chance. Those who interviewed Dennis Nilsen in custody described him as a rather dour and strangely colourless character. He didn't have the mystique or dark charisma of some other famous serial killers.

Dennis Nilsen told the police that he was happy to have been caught because he was rather hoping they could tell him why he had become a serial killer. Nilsen said that his arrest was the day that 'help' arrived. While many serial killers are reluctant to speak about their crimes or (ludicrously) maintain their innocence, Dennis Nilsen loved to talk about his murders and would discuss them for hours if given the chance. He seemed to crave attention. After he was arrested, Dennis Nilsen boasted that he was the 'murderer of the century'. Oddly, Dennis Nilsen seemed delighted to be famous all of a sudden - even if he did have to murder a dozen people to achieve this fame.

During his police interviews after his arrest, Dennis Nilsen said that he sometimes left a dead body in a chair before he went to work because that meant he had someone to come home to in the evening. When he was arrested, the formal questioning of Dennis Nilsen lasted for 30 hours (it was spread out over several days). Nilsen drew some sketches of his victims for the police to help with identification. You can find these strange and childlike illustrations online. While elements of institutional homophobia in the Met meant that early complaints against Dennis Nilsen were not given the credence and importance they deserved, the actual investigation once Nilsen was arrested was highly efficient and professional.

When he was questioned by the police, a detective told Dennis Nilsen he was a predator with evil intent. Nilsen replied - "I seek company first, and hope everything will be all right." The police who interviewed Nilsen described him as a bore. They almost suspected that Dennis Nilsen had become a serial killer because that was the only way he could get the world to pay him any attention. Detective Chief Inspector Peter Jay, who arrested Dennis Nilsen, did not believe that Nilsen was mentally ill. Jay simply found Nilsen to be a strange but cunning and coldly calculating man. After his arrest, Nilsen wrote a note for the police in which he proposed a bizarre (not to mention ludicrous) motive for his murders - 'It may be a perverted overkill of my need to help people – victims who I decide to release quickly from the slings and arrows of their outrageous fortune, pain and suffering.'

Dennis Nilsen told the police that he had been concerned about catching a disease from the dead bodies stored in his flat. He was well aware that he wasn't exactly adhering to public health standards. The police found that Dennis Nilsen still had the tie he used to strangle Stephen Sinclair. During his police interview, Nilsen joked that he was out of ties and only had a clip-on one left. This was a sick attempt at black humour. When the police asked Dennis Nilsen how many bodies he had under the floorboards he replied - "I didn't do a stock check." Dennis Nilsen had the disturbing ability to talk about the most gruesome and harrowing deeds in a calm matter of fact way and even make jokes.

It has been speculated that Nilsen claimed to have killed fifteen people at first so he would have a greater kill count than Peter Sutcliffe. This is pure speculation but with a man possessed of Nilsen's huge ego you never know. Although Nilsen revised his kill count to twelve, police officers who worked on the case didn't believe him. They think he killed more than he let on. The police officers who questioned Nilsen after his arrest were as polite as possible and gave him all the snacks and cigarettes he wanted. This was designed to make him more willing to talk and confess. The tactic worked. The police who interviewed Nilsen found it rather chilling that he didn't seem at all affected by having to describe the things he had done. Nilsen displayed no sense of remorse or any emotion in these interviews.

There were a number of unverified victims of Nilsen. One of the victims that Nilsen could provide very few details on was described by him to the police as a 'long haired hippie'. Dennis Nilsen said that his fifth victim was a male prostitute who was either from the Philippines or Thailand. One of the other victims that Nilsen couldn't remember the name of was apparently a skinhead he took back to his flat. Nilsen was very careful in his selection of victims. He chose people who he knew would probably not be missed or reported as missing straight away. It is a common tactic for serial killers to target transient victims.

Nielsen said to a police psychiatrist of his victims that - "They would sit down. I would talk incessantly like an auctioneer. Outpourings about music, politics, Margaret Thatcher etc. All completely cynical. If they entered into it, they would be OK. If they were sleeping, they would be dead already. It was the ultimate reply to apathy." This was a rather chilling statement because it implied that Nilsen would kill people who mildly irritated him. We know that Nilsen's youngest victim was fourteen and that he was once accused of indecently assaulting a ten year-old boy. Nilsen also said he once had sexual contact with an underage boy David Gallichan brought home. With this in mind its seems highly likely that, if he hadn't been caught, Nilsen might have murdered some children in the end.

After he was arrested in 1983, the Daily Mirror reported that a mystery female friend of Nilsen had telephoned him two days before he was taken into custody. The woman was alleged to have packed a suitcase for Nilsen. Although the police asked this woman to come forward and go to the police station she never turned up. This story therefore remains a mystery and was possibly fabricated or simply not true. There is no evidence that Nilsen ever hatched any sort of plan to escape.

After he was arrested, Nilsen had to go with the police to 195 Melrose Avenue and show them where he had buried things and lit bonfires. Most of the bone fragments the police later found at Melrose Avenue were blackened from Nilsen's attempt to burn them on a bonfire. It was absolutely freezing weather when Nilsen was arrested. The police who had to dig up his old garden had a most unpleasant task. They had to use a hosepipe to sift through the mud and the water was ice cold. There were many bones found in the garden out the back of Nilsen's first flat. After he burned the bodies he would try to smash the bones but he'd obviously missed a few. The police also found a lot of teeth fragments in the garden at Melrose Avenue after Nilsen was arrested. More than 1,000 pieces of flesh and bone were found by forensic teams and police officers at the two London flats Dennis Nilsen had lived in.

When the police searched the garden at Melrose Avenue after Nilsen's arrest, they found men's clothing and an old chequebook that had been partially burned. The police searching the Melrose Avenue garden out the back of where Nilsen had lived also found a thigh bone and a jaw bone. It has been alleged that Nilsen once even tried to dispose of some human remains in a local cemetery. Dennis Nilsen said he had so little space left when he killed Malcolm Barlow (the last Melrose Avenue victim in 1981) that he stuffed the body under the sink. The police who had to dig up the garden where Nilsen lived at Melrose Avenue found a decomposing foot in a sock in one place. Nilsen said that by the time he got around to dissecting the bodies of the victims there wasn't too much blood because they had already been dead for a while.

Dennis Nilsen, oddly, seemed to give the impression to the police that his abuse of the corpses was trivial and unimportant because the real crime had been murder. This was a bizarre way of looking at things. In notes written after his arrest, Nilsen said 'There is no disputing the fact that I am a violent killer under certain circumstances. The victim is the dirty platter after the feast, and the washing up is a clinically ordinary task. It would be better if my reason for killing could be clearly defined, ie robbery, jealousy, hate, revenge, sex, blood lust or sadism. But it is none of these.'

We know that Dennis Nilsen let some people go even though he could have killed them if he had wanted to. It is, as we have noted, rare for serial killers to display mercy like this. One could not imagine, for example, Ted Bundy allowing a woman he had at his mercy to go free. Nilsen was a rather complex serial killer to understand at times. He didn't conform to some of the common patterns we see in other killers. In other instances though, Nilsen was a lot like serial killers who had gone before him. Nilsen wasn't exactly the first person to strangle people and sexually abuse their corpses.

Dennis Nilsen seemed surprised that people who interviewed him found it strange that this seemingly placid man had the ability to kill and dissect bodies. Nilsen was genuinely odd in that he wasn't insane but, all the same, didn't seem to comprehend that he had done some grotesque and harrowing things. Dennis Nilsen once wrote - 'The population at large is neither 'ordinary' or 'normal'. They seem to be bound together by a collective ignorance of themselves and what they are. They have, every one of them, got their deep dark thoughts with many a skeleton rattling in their secret cupboards. Their fascination with 'types' like myself plagues them with the mystery of why and how a living person can actually do things which may be only those dark images and acts secretly within them. I believe they can identify with these 'dark images and acts' and loathe anything which reminds them of this dark side of themselves.'

After the police arrested Dennis Nilsen they had to call a press conference quite soon because Mike Cattran (the Dyno-Rod man) had spoken to a local reporter and Fleet Street were now aware that a very big story was brewing in relation to Cranley Gardens. The police didn't want Fleet Street to publish too much about Dennis Nilsen in case it harmed the investigation so the police press conference was an attempt to control the release of information. The police questioning of Nilsen after his arrest was intensive and extensive. They needed to charge him with something as soon as possible so that reporting on the case would be forbidden until the trial. The fact that Nilsen gave the police the name of a victim early after his arrest was a relief for them because it meant they could detain him in custody.

After he was arrested, Nilsen was visited in prison by the union rep at the Jobcentre he used to work in. She told Nilsen that she would not believe the allegations against him unless they were proved in court. Nilsen resigned from his position as a civil servant to save the Jobcentre from any embarrassment while he was awaiting his trial. It's not as if he was likely to go back to work anyway. He had already confessed to several murders! Dennis Nilsen didn't really have much choice when it came to his confession. He could hardly say that he had no idea how all these bodies had ended up in his attic flat!

For his first court hearing at Highbury Magistrates Court, Dennis Nilsen eschewed the traditional blanket over the head (a custom for notorious criminals entering the building). Nilsen said that he didn't want to 'hide' like a common criminal. In 2014, a letter titled Mental Condition Notes that Dennis Nilsen had written six weeks after he was arrested came to light. In the letter, Nilsen said that he was glad to have been captured and blamed alcohol on releasing 'dormant' demons within him.

Nilsen claimed that when he sobered up after a murder he felt remorse and wished he hadn't killed anyone. However, although he said that he needed alcohol to kill and dissect and had a drink problem, medical tests after his arrest showed no sign of alcohol withdrawal or alcoholism in Dennis Nilsen. These murders could not be blamed on alcohol. That was far too simplistic and gave a cold killer like Dennis Nilsen far too much credit. Dennis Nilsen later seemed to acknowledge this and said in prison that it was addiction to the 'ritual' of killing and not alcohol that had made him a murderer.

THE COMPANY KILLER

Brixton Prison, where Nilsen went after his arrest, was a pretty rough place but it was actually a step-up compared to the squalid conditions that Nilsen lived in at Cranley Gardens. When he was arrested and sent to Brixton Prison, Nilsen said he was shocked by the racism of the prison staff towards black prisoners. David Wilson, now a professor of criminology, met Dennis Nilsen while working for the prison service at Brixton. He described Nilsen in the flesh as seeming like a 'weedy geography teacher'. David Wilson didn't believe that Nilsen was insane. "There was no evidence of mental illness, he was interested in power and control and the ultimate form of expressing that was through taking other people's lives." Ted Bundy said he felt like a God when he took a life and this was addictive. Dennis Nilsen said something similar.

While he was awaiting trial, Nilsen spent some time in the prison hospital as he was deemed a suicide risk. Dennis Nilsen, ludicrously, complained of being kept in prison with other inmates while he was awaiting trial. He seemed to believe he was harmless and should have some sort of special arrangement. When he was at Brixton Prison, Nilsen was outraged when he was banned from the chapel. The governor thought that Nilsen's presence might cause a fuss. It was a blow to Nilsen because although he wasn't religious anymore he liked to go to the chapel simply to break up the monotony of his cell and the drab prison surroundings.

After he was arrested, Nilsen was seen with a Complete Works of Shakespeare in prison. This felt like an affectation because there was little evidence in his flat that he enjoyed literature. Nilsen once asked a prison officer what he was supposed to do with his cigarette butts because he didn't have an ashtray. Nilsen was told to flush them down the toilet and replied - "The last time I put anything down the toilet I got into trouble." Nilsen claimed that he spent a lot of time in solitary confinement while awaiting his trial. Dennis Nilsen said that going to prison was strangely comforting in a way. It was the first time in years that he had been surrounded by people and not isolated - apart from solitary confinement anyway.

While he was in Brixton Prison awaiting trial, Dennis Nilsen would sometimes help other inmates to write letters home. Though no rocket scientist himself, Nilsen found that he was pretty intelligent compared to most of the other prison inmates. Nilsen went on a hunger strike at one point. He also had a period where he refused to wear his prison uniform. Nilsen also began corresponding with the writer Brian Masters after his arrest. Masters then interviewed Nilsen in prison and in 1985 wrote the most famous book about this notorious killer - Killing For Company. Nilsen wrote reams of notes for the police and Brian Masters. Some of these notes were completely irrelevant to his case and simply featured Nilsen ranting about subjects like politics.

Some of the tabloids had dubbed Nilsen The Kindly Killer because it was reported that he would cook a meal for his victims. The 'meal' though never amounted to much more than an omelette - if that. There was never much evidence that Nilsen cooked at home. The title of the book by Masters was much more apt. Nilsen truly was The Company Killer because that was the motivation for his murders. He wanted some company and dead people suited him just fine because they could never talk back and never leave. Nilsen killed for company.

When Brian Masters first met Dennis Nilsen in prison, Nilsen never asked him any questions and simply spoke at him. This was Nilsen's way of trying to assert dominance in their relationship. Masters wrote of his first encounter with Dennis Nilsen - 'From the letters we had exchanged, I expected someone who was sensitive and introspective. At our first meeting, however, I saw an assertive man, bristling with confidence and swagger, amazingly relaxed as he slouched with an arm over the back of his chair, totally in command and behaving as if he were interviewing me for a job. He gave an impression of intellectual intensity, coupled with a surprising truculence. I soon learned that this was a radical political streak exaggerated by his having to spend countless hours confined with nobody to speak to.'

Brian Masters said that Dennis Nilsen would always hold your gaze and stare directly at the person he was talking to. There was never anything 'shifty' or evasive about his body language. Masters suggested that Nilsen deliberately moved to a flat (Cranley Gardens) with no garden access or floorboards in the end as a means to try and stop himself from killing or get captured. With no way to dispose of body parts (save for flushing them down the toilet), Nilsen must have known he was on borrowed time.

Brian Masters said that he asked the police if he could view the photographic evidence of what they found in Nilsen's flat and former garden. However, it was so grisly and unpleasant that he couldn't view all of the photographs. Masters said that when he wrote his book about Dennis Nilsen there were some details he left out because they were simply too disgusting to put into print. Brian Masters said that "He (Nilsen) would put into the garden, the spleen and stuff which might prove impossible to live with, and then put what was left of the corpse under the floorboards."

In his book, Brian Masters said that one time when Nilsen was burning remains of some victims on a huge bonfire, some local children were attracted by the bonfire and started dancing around it. Brian Masters also said that Dennis Nilsen once said to him - "You know, you'd be surprised how heavy a human head is when you pick it up by the hair."

Nilsen told Brian Masters that he killed because he enjoyed it. Nilsen later tried to retract this statement and say it wasn't true and he hadn't meant it. Nilsen once told a psychiatrist - "God only knows what thoughts go through my mind when it is captive within a destructive binge."

Brian Masters said in his book Killing For Company that Dennis Nilsen would 'Even would go so far as to come home from work and find the corpses sitting in the same armchair that he'd left them in that morning [and would say] to them 'Guess what happened to me today?'.' Brian Masters also said in his book that Dennis Nilsen's mother was first told what her son had done by a reporter. The reporter secretly had a tape recorder in his pocket so that he could capture her live reaction to learning that her son was a serial killer. The relationship between Masters and Dennis Nilsen would endure for quite a time to come but it would fracture in the end. Dennis Nilsen was not an easy person to get on with - even in prison.

Brian Masters had never written about serial killers before he worked on his Dennis Nilsen book. One of his motivations was that, as a gay man himself, he didn't like the way that the tabloids were using the Nilsen case to somehow connect being gay with murder and depravity. You'd think all gay men were depraved necrophile predators trawling the dark underbelly of London for victims if you believed half the stuff in the tabloids at the time. Masters thought this coverage was rather silly and very offensive. Unfortunately though, the case of Dennis Nilsen is not only an unbelievable tale of real life horror but also a dark slice of social history.

During the killing spree of Dennis Nilsen, the police plainly did not deduce that a serial killer was targeting gay men in North London. Because they were gay and in some cases on the fringes of society (in that they were transient and poor), Nilsen's victims might as well have been invisible. At least two men escaped from Nilsen but didn't bother to go to the police because they knew the Met wouldn't do anything.

In their experience, the police did not involve themselves in incidents involving gay men because of institutional homophobia. The police were not interested in the 'lover's tiffs' of gay men and, as a consequence, failed to investigate an active serial killer. Compare this to the case of Peter Sutcliffe and the Ripper murders. In that case the women of Bradford quite rightly made their voices heard and put pressure on the police to find the perpetrator of the murders. Gay men in the London of the late seventies and early eighties had no such influence. It is very shocking to think that in the late seventies and early eighties the police were disinterested in a case where a gay man is reporting that someone just tried to strangle them.

There is sometimes a tendency to think that a disproportionate percentage of serial killers are gay. This is probably a consequence of famous gay serial killers like Nilsen, Jeffrey Dahmer, and John Wayne Gacy. Studies show though that the overwhelming majority of serial killers are heterosexual. This tends to make the most notorious gay serial killers more famous. They aren't quite as common. There have been though a number of gay serial killers both before Nilsen and after him. Some (though not all) display common themes and conduct with Nilsen.

Stephen Port is a rapist and killer who murdered four men in London from 2014 to 2015. He would drug them with GBH (gamma-Hydroxybutyric acid - known as a 'date rape' drug). Three of the victims were disposed of in a graveyard by Port. He was given life in prison. Stephen Port, who worked as a chef in a bus depot, once appeared on television as a kitchen assistant in the popular BBC show Masterchef. The BBC have now edited him out of that episode. Port was a very dangerous and ruthless man. He was overwhelmed by his fantasy of having sex with victims who were inert or helpless (this is, as we have noted, a common heme in serial killers). Port even faked suicide notes for some of his victims and this made the police slow in connecting the deaths. Port met his victims through online dating apps and this case led to some understandable concern over their safety.

Ronald Dominique was born in Thibodaux, Louisiana, in 1964. He is known as The Bayou Strangler. Dominique grew up on a trailer park in a poor family but he was a decent student and sang in the choir. However, he was very short and always overweight and this led to bullying and Dominique feeling like an outcast in society. Dominique realised at quite a young age that he was gay but this was something he found difficult to cope with. When he tried to secretly visit a gay bar as a teenager some homophobic kids found about about this and taunted him. It's safe to say that Ronald Dominique was one of those people who often felt like he didn't fit in anywhere.

Dominique studied computer science at college but dropped out before he completed his course. He struggled to hold down a job and so, with money tight, sometimes lived with relatives to save rent for a time. In 1996, Dominique was arrested after a half-naked man jumped out of his apartment window and claimed that Dominique had raped him and then attempted to murder him. However, Dominique evaded the rap for this when the man could not be located for a court case and full legal process.

Dominique was arrested again soon after when a woman said he punched her in the face during a parking dispute. The case against him was dropped though because he offered an apology and came to an agreement with the woman. Around this time, Dominique was living a fairly aimless sort of life. In his spare time he sang in a gay bar as a Patti LaBelle impersonator. However, Dominique, the ultimate outsider, didn't feel at home in the gay community and failed to establish any meaningful relationships with gay men.

Ronald Dominique's murder spree began in 1997. He later confessed to the rape and murder of at least 23 men. The crimes took place in the Terrebonne, Lafourche, Iberville, St. Charles and Jefferson parishes in suburban New Orleans and the victims were aged between 16 and 46. Dominique would pick up a lot of men in gay bars and offer them money for sex. Sometimes he would even approach straight men and offer them money if they would have sex with his (fictitious) girlfriend. He drove around in a van and would take victims to his trailer. Once he had overpowered them or incapacitated them he would then rape and strangle the victim before dumping the body.

Some of the victims were found to have been tied and bound before they died and there was evidence that some of them had been heavily struck in the head with a blunt object. A number of the victims were homeless people. Dominique was one of those serial killers who was obsessed with a dark fantasy of sexually abusing someone who was helpless. He, like so many killers, decided that he could only act on this fantasy in real life if there were no living victims left to blow the whistle on him.

Dominique's killing spree came to an end when a man named Ricky Wallace contacted the police and reported Dominique. He told the police that Dominique had once lured him to his trailer with the promise of a sexual encounter with his girlfriend but when he got there it was simply Dominique alone. Dominique had then tried to tie him up in a bondage game. Wallace's instincts told him that Ronald Dominique was dangerous so he left. When the police investigated Ronald Dominique they connected his DNA to two murders and he soon confessed to others. Dominique pleaded guilty to first-degree murder in a deal to avoid the death penalty. He was given eight life sentences and is now incarcerated at the Louisiana State Penitentiary.

Dean Corll was born in 1939 in Fort Wayne, Indiana. Dean Corll was a former US Army repairman who killed at least 22 young men and boys between 1970 and 1973. Corll was a sadistic and evil man who would torture his victims for days. He was able to win the trust of his victims because he had two teenage accomplices - Wayne Henley and David Brooks. The really strange thing about Corll is that he didn't come from the nightmarish backdrop that many serial killers seemed to have to endure as children. Corll's mother owned a company that made candy and they were successful and fairly wealthy. Corll worked for the family candy company and was popular in the community. People who met him thought that he was a nice man. It's true what they say though. Appearances can be very deceptive.

With the help of Wayne Henley and David Brooks, Corll lured many boys and male teenagers to his house in Houston. The victims were told that there was going to be a party with food, drink, and drugs. This usually proved sufficient motivation for them to take the bait. What awaited them though was a nightmare. Once they were vulnerable, Corll would restrain the victims, handcuff them, and then sexually abuse and torture them. When he was satisfied he would kill them by strangulation or simply shoot them.

Many of Dean Corll's victims were disposed of via boat shed on Sam Rayburn Reservoir. It is strongly suspected that he killed many more people than the authorities are officially aware of. Corll would make his victims write letters and postcards addressed to their relatives so that he could post them at a later date (when the victims were dead) and make it less likely his victims would be reported as missing. Many young men and kids had gone missing in the Houston area during this time and the culprit was the evil Dean Corll.

His killing spree though came to a sudden and violent end in 1973. Wayne Henley eventually decided he couldn't go on with what he was part of and shot Corll dead. Henley and Brooks then turned themselves in to the police and were given life in prison. Henley and Brooks tried (in vain) to argue in their trials that it was Corll who had actually done the murders. This was technically true but they had facilitated the murders by luring the victims. They had effectively given these boys a death sentence by taking them to Corll's house.

It is truly terrifying to think of how many people Dean Corll might have murdered had he not been shot dead. No one suspected him of anything because he was friendly and popular in the community and hid his secret life of picking up boys for sex. The candy company was like the perfect disguise. Corll was even known to give out free candy to local children.

He was literally the last person in Houston anyone would suspect of being a sick serial killer.

To this day we still don't know how many people Corll really killed. The process of identifying potential victims from missing persons reports still continues. Detective David Mullican said of Corll - "How that man was able to go out to that storage shed, time after time, and bury one more dead boy is something I'll never understand. You get close to evil like that, no matter how long ago it was, and it never leaves you." Dean Corll is rather inevitably often dubbed The Candy Man in true crime retrospectives of his case today. He was one of the most sadistic and evil killers imaginable.

Fritz Haarmann was born in Hanover, Germany in 1879. In true crime circles he is known as The Vampire of Hanover for reasons we'll get to very soon. Haarmann was an unhappy child (what else is new when it comes to serial killers?) and seemed to have a lifelong bitterness at his father. He suffered seizures when he was a boy and it is speculated that these might have left some lasting damage that impaired his mental health. He went to a military academy (in those days Germany was a very militaristic nation) but was kicked out because they didn't think he was healthy enough to make a good student or potential soldier.

After this, Haarmann got married (although he was secretly gay) and picked up some work at a shipping docks. Money was still tight though and he became a petty thief - which earned him a short spell in prison. It was after his release from prison that Haarmann seemed to completely snap and become a deranged serial killer. His victims were the usual serial killer targets. Prostitutes, runaways, homeless people. All of his victims were boys or men. Haarmann would lure the victims back to his home with promises of food and drink. When they were vulnerable he would bite them in the throat in savage fashion. He referred to this as a 'love bite'.

If this 'love bite' hadn't killed them then Haarmann would

finish them off by strangulation. Haarmann would keep any possessions his victims had and sell them on the black market. This wasn't the only thing he sold on the black market. He also sold meat. Could this meat have been the human flesh of his victims? That doesn't seem unlikely at all. Fritz Haarmann was no rocket scientist when it came to brains though. He wasn't exactly the most adept serial killer when it came to covering the tracks of his grisly deeds.

Haarmann had been dumping his victims in the Leine River (a river in Thuringia and Lower Saxony). Some of the bodies washed ashore - which led the police to investigate the river thoroughly. They dragged the river and found hundreds of human bones. From what they found the police estimated that there were over twenty victims at least in this river. Haarmann, because of his criminal history, ended up on a list of suspects and was placed under secret observation by the police. They saw him trying to pick up boys at the train station and decided to search his home. Haarmann's home was full of blood stains and he was swiftly arrested.

The trial of Fritz Haarmann took place in 1924. It didn't last very long. He was found guilty of 24 murders and sentenced to death by beheading. Haarmann's lover Hans Grans was also sentenced to death. Grans knew of the murders and had even ended up with the possessions of some of the victims as gifts. The trial had a huge number of witnesses called to give evidence. Some of the neighbours of Haarmann testified that they had seen him carrying large sacks to the river at strange hours. Haarmann made a very full confession to the police anyway. He gave detailed and gruesome details on how he had used an axe and knives to dismember his victims after death. On April the 15th 1925, Fritz Haarmann was beheaded by Guillotine in the grounds of Hanover Prison. His last words were - "I repent, but I do not fear death."

Larry Eyler was born in Crawfordsville, Indiana in 1952. He tends to be known as The Highway Killer or The Interstate Killer. Eyler had a succession of different stepfathers as a child who he said all treated him badly. Larry Eyler was gay but (like other serial killers it seems) struggled to come to terms with his sexuality. He was a pretty poor student by all accounts and dropped out of high school and some colleges. His early jobs included a stint as a security guard and an employee in a shoe store.

Eyler later became a house painter, worked at a liquor store weekends, and seemed to settle into the gay scene of Indianapolis fairly well. He was into bodybuilding and lived with a science professor named Robert David Little in what was apparently a purely platonic friendship and not a relationship. Eyler was though in a sexual relationship with a young man named John Dobrovolskis - despite the fact that Dobrovolskis was married with children.

In 1978, there was an incident where Eyler stabbed a hitchhiker but he somehow evaded serious charges. He simply pled guilty and received a small fine. This same year though he would begin his murder spree. The incident with the hitchhiker is seen retrospectively as something of a 'test run' for Eyler. It seems plausible that he was trying to kill this man. Eyler's murders took place in the Midwest. He would drive around in his pickup truck and target hitchhikers and male prostitutes. His victims were usually drugged (he would put sedatives in alcohol) and bound and then stabbed or beaten to death. One victim was stabbed 32 times.

Eyler seemed to have a strange and sick fetish for inflicting stab wounds to the chest and abdomen of his victims. Some of the victims were disembowelled after their death. The bodies of the victims were often found in fields near the highway and nearly always had their pants round their ankles. One victim was found on a farm and traces of human flesh on the wall of a barn led the police to suspect that the victim had been forcibly pinned on the wall and tortured. Larry Eyler was a very evil and out of control killer. Like a number of other serial killers, he also liked to take photographs of his victims.

As the body count piled up, the authorities had obviously deduced that there was definite pattern to these murders. A special task force was set up in an attempt to catch the killer. The police were eventually contacted by a man named Thomas Henderson who told them he suspected Larry Eyler of being the killer because Eyler was known to be obsessed by bondage games and also had an arrest from back in 1978 (when he stabbed the hitchhiker).

Henderson also told the police that Eyler had also once drugged and molested a fourteen year-old boy. At this point, Eyler was not arrested but he was placed under a degree of police surveillance. Meanwhile, bodies that matched the modus operandi of the killer continued to be found. Eyler was arrested for the first time late in 1983 when a police officer noticed his truck parked in a rural spot and found him in the vehicle with a bound man. Eyler had surgical tape and a knife in the car.

Eyler refused to discuss his sexuality with the police but they impounded his vehicle and found a large amount of incriminating evidence against him. Although he was not immediately charged with anything and even released, Eyler must have known his days were numbered. As the police investigation against him continued he sued them for harassment and 'psychological warfare'. Eyler was eventually arrested and charged but - unbelievably - the evidence against him was found inadmissible (obtained without probable cause) and he was released.

Eyler moved to Chicago and (of course) went back to killing again. He murdered a sixteen year-old male prostitute named Daniel Bridges and dumped the body (which Eyler had gruesomely dissected) near a garbage dumpster. The decision to release Eyler had cost Daniel Bridges his young life. The police, on hearing reports that Eyler lived in the area and was seen dumping trash near that dumpster, arrested him and found evidence of blood and bloodstained clothes in his apartment. Eyler had painted the apartment in an attempt to hide the blood but this ruse hadn't worked.

Larry Eyler was now charged with the murder of Daniel Bridges. He denied the charges but was found guilty and sentenced to death by lethal injection. A number of appeals and further murder convictions followed. Larry Eyler died in 1994 from AIDS-related complications. Upon his death, his attorney Kathleen Zellner revealed a confession that Eyler had asked her to read out posthumously. In this, Eyler confessed to 17 murders and said he had killed four other people with David Little (the professor he had lived with). The first part of Eyler's confession was too conservative (in terms of victims) and the second part was complete fiction. Little was completely innocent. The complete victims of Larry Eyler have yet to all be identified and named. It may take a long time for that to happen.

Patrick Wayne Kearney was born in East Los Angeles in 1939. Patrick Wayne Kearney is probably one of the worst American serial killers in terms of numbers. He confessed to 35 murders but the true figure is most likely considerably higher. Kearney is sometimes known as The Trash Bag Killer in true crime biographies. This is because he would dismember his victims into trash bags and dump them by the side of the road or put them in the desert.

Kearney had fantasies about killing people from a young age. He was not only a killer but a necrophile too. He was married as a very young man but the marriage was a sham because Kearney was gay. After the marriage collapsed (which didn't take very long at all), Kearney spent most of his spare time trawling the underbelly of the gay scene. His victims were mostly young men but he killed boys too. Kearney worked as an engineer for Hughes Aircraft and managed to hide his dark side from colleagues. He claimed to have killed for the first time in 1962.

In the late 1960s, Kearney acquired a younger lover named David Hill. The pair had first met in the armed forces. They would argue a lot and Kearney would take long drives to clear his head after their arguments. These long drives soon began to involve him killing hitchhikers. It is speculated that a separation between Kearney and Hill might have been the trigger for Kearney's more prolific killings in the early 1970s. At one point he was killing people at a rate of one victim a month. It is said that Kearney was bullied a lot as a child and that he often tried to kill victims who reminded him of the childhood bullies who once made his life such a misery.

Kearney was only 5'5 tall and not the most physically imposing man. For this reason he used a gun and would shoot his victims dead while they were asleep or sitting in the car passenger seat next to him. He would then drive to a secluded spot and sexually abuse the body. Many of his victims were hitchhikers. Kearney, with his short stature and spectacles, wouldn't have seemed any threat at all to these victims. He often wore a tie too so seemed perfectly respectable and normal at first glance. Kearney said he would sometimes punch and kick the bodies of victims because he found this cathartic. He would slice up the victims to satisfy himself and then dismember the body with a hacksaw and knife.

Kearney was quite a shrewd killer. He once removed a bullet from the head of one of victims so it would not be traced to his gun. He dumped a lot of his victims in the desert to be eaten by birds and animals. Kearney would sometimes wash his victims too to remove any potential forensic evidence. His youngest victim was only five years-old. Kearney's last verified victim was John Otis LaMay in 1977. LaMay had been shot and sexually abused.

The police found the remains of LeMay and then learned that the victim had last been seen with Kearney and David Hill. Kearney and Hill fled to Texas but they were apprehended in the end. Kearney confessed to 35 murders while Hill was cleared of having any involvement in the deaths. It was Kearney alone who had murdered all of these people. Kearney pled guilty to avoid the death penalty and got twenty-one life sentences. As part of his deal he had to agree to help the police find as many victim remains as possible. The judge who convicted Patrick Wayne Kearney called him an 'insult' to humanity.

John Wayne Gacy was born in Chicago in 1942. Gacy is one of the most evil serial killers in the history of the United States (and given the competition that's really saying something). Gacy's childhood was unhappy by all accounts thanks to his strict father. He claimed too that he was molested as a child. Gacy worked as a mortician's assistant as a very young man and later seemed to confess that he had once fondled one of the corpses there. Although he had a wife and family, John Wayne Gacy was secretly gay. His family man image was useful though as a sort of disguise. When he got married, Gacy worked for a shoe company and was involved in The United States Junior Chamber (the Jaycees). This was a leadership training and civic organization for people between the ages of 18 and 40.

As a young man, Gacy had worked as assistant precinct captain for a Democratic Party candidate in his neighborhood. The ability of serial killers to blend into society and appear normal is often called the mask of sanity. The mask worn by Gacy was very elaborate and convincing. He was once even introduced to the First Lady Rosalynn Carter at a function for the Democratic Party. Gacy changed occupations when he became the manager of a Kentucky Fried Chicken franchise. He was very successful in this and had a natural flair for business and promotion. However, the image he projected to the community as a generous family man and solid citizen was simply a facade. Gacy's secret life was dark and disturbing. In the late 1960s, Gacy sexually assaulted a fifteen year-old boy named Donald Vorhees. Gacy then gave another boy some money to beat up Vorhees so that he would be too intimidated to testify in a court.

The incident with Vorhees was far from isolated. Gacy had sexual relations with many teenagers and boys and he didn't really care about consent. Donald Vorhees refused to be intimidated though and told the police about Gacy. Gacy was sentenced to ten years in prison for underage sexual assualt but he was such a model prisoner he was out on parole after a couple of years. The ability of Gacy to charm and fool the authorities into thinking he was a decent man was - tragically - something he would put into practice with his future victims. The authorities, sadly, seemed to somewhat lose track of Gacy after his release. He was able to go back into the community without it being public knowledge that he was a convicted sex offender. He lived with his mother for a while and then got engaged so that he could have have a new family. This new relationship gave Gacy two stepdaughters.

Gacy started a construction business and purchased a house in Norwood Park Township, an unincorporated area of Cook County. The address of John Wayne Gacy was 8213 W. Summerdale Ave. The construction business was a big success and made Gacy financially secure. Once again, Gacy was playing a role he loved - that of the solid citizen and pillar of the community. He was even dressing up as a clown to entertain the local children. John Wayne Gacy actually had two different personas when he dressed up as a clown. Sometimes he was Pogo the Clown and sometimes he was Patches the Clown. These two 'characters' had their own costume. It comes as no great surprise then to learn that Gacy would become forever known as The Clown Killer. From this point on he became one of the worst serial killers in history.

Gacy murdered 33 teenage boys and young men between 1972 and 1978. John Wayne Gacy's access to victims was provided by his construction business. He was constantly in contact with teenagers and young men looking for some temporary work. One of John Wayne Gacy's methods of getting his victims handcuffed was to pretend he was demonstrating a magic trick. He would escape from the handcuffs himself and then challenge the victim to do the same. Gacy would usually try and get his victims a bit drunk for this game. By the time they realised it was not a game and that Gacy was dangerous it was all too late. They were already helpless. John Wayne Gacy weighed 230 pounds. He was a big man who would have been difficult to fight off - especially if one was restrained.

John Wayne Gacy stuffed the bodies of most of his victims in the crawlspace of his home. When his wife asked about the smell he told her it was mice. Gacy used his experience as a mortician's assistant to block the cavities of his victims with rags and underwear. This prevented too much leakage after death. John Wayne Gacy would sometimes contact the police and report one of the men he had killed as missing. This was a tactic designed to make him seem trustworthy and throw the police off his scent.

Gacy drove a black Oldsmobile Delta 88. He liked this car because it had a big trunk. When his crawlspace started to get too full up with bodies, he used his car to throw dead victims off the I-55 bridge into the Des Plaines River. Gacy got divorced around this time and so had more privacy and time to himself - which was obviously a recipe for disaster when it comes serial killers. He was completely out of control. However, at long last, the authorities had finally started to take an interest in Gacy again.

A teenager named Robert Priest was reported missing and the police, upon further investigation, deduced that one of the last things Priest had done before he vanished was to visit John Wayne Gacy to talk about a job. The police, investigating Gacy further, now discovered the sexual assault conviction that had landed him in prison years ago. Further evidence against Gacy came from a young man named Jeffrey Rignal. The police learned that Rignal had accused Gacy of drugging and raping him.

The police decided to place Gacy under surveillance while they tried to build a case against him. John Wayne Gacy was very arrogant and full of bluster and bravado when he deduced that the police had him under surveillance. He liked to invite any detectives trailing him to breakfast. However, time was fast running out for this awful man. When the police obtained the legal right to search his house the game was finally up for Gacy. The crawlspace in his house was one of the most disturbing sights these detectives were ever likely to witness. Some of the bodies had become fused together in decomposition. Many of John Wayne Gacy's victims were found to have rope tied around their neck. It was an exceptionally complex and time consuming task to identify all of the victims. Sadly, to this day, there are still victims of Gacy yet to be identified.

Gacy was sentenced to death for the twelve counts of murder and spent fourteen years on Death Row. Gacy spent most of his time in prison painting. He liked to paint Elvis, Jesus, skulls, and Disney characters. Gacy naturally did a few self-portraits too - complete with clown costume. Gacy is said to have done 2,000 paintings while he was on Death Row. The Tatou Art Gallery in Beverly Hills tried to sell some of John Wayne Gacy's paintings. They were described as art brut. Legend has it that Johnny Depp owns one of Gacy's paintings. Two businessmen eventually purchased many of John Wayne Gacy's prison paintings in the end and had them destroyed in a mass bonfire where people (including relatives of Gacy's victims) gathered and cheered.

Gacy was killed by lethal injection in May, 1994. Gacy was allowed to have a last picnic with his family before his execution. For his last meal Gacy requested 12 fried shrimp, a bucket of original recipe KFC, french fries, and strawberries. John Wayne Gacy's last words before his execution were said to be - kiss my ass. He then taunted the police by saying they would never find all of the bodies. After his death, John Wayne Gacy's Pogo the Clown costume was put on display at the Alcatraz East crime museum. Gacy told the authorities that he had four personalities. The contractor, clown, politician, and then plain Jack Hanley. Jack Hanley, said Gacy, was the serial killer.

Robert Andrew Berdella was born in 1949, in Cuyahoga Falls,

Ohio. Berdella was a serial killer who restrained, tortured, and killed at least six men from 1984 to 1987 in Kansas City, Missouri. He was known as The Kansas City Butcher. Berdella was said to be rather aloof and detached as a child. He had a brother who he always felt overshadowed by because his brother was athletic and good at sport while he wasn't. Berdella was quite dumpy and wore thick glasses.

Berdella deduced he was gay from a very young age but he struggled to come to terms with his sexuality and didn't admit to it for a long time. As a teenager he even had a few girlfriends in an attempt to disguise his real self. His father died when he was a relatively young man and this is said to have made him even more aloof and withdrawn. Berdella didn't like the fact that his mother then remarried. Berdella's hobbies were collecting stamps, strange art, and antiques. In the early eighties he used his collection to start a business. Berdella ran a booth at a market called Bob's Bizarre Bizarre which sold oddities and antiques. It is sometimes suggested that he might sold some of the skulls of his victims at this booth.

Berdella studied art at college but dropped out in the end. During this period he was busted on drugs charges a few times. One of the drugs he used was the mind altering LSD. Despite this, Berdella seemed - on the outside - to be doing quite well. He was popular in the community in which he lived and, in addition to the business he started, got work as a chef. Berdella seemed to befriend a lot of runaways and male prostitutes. He claimed to be a sort of mentor to them and said he was helping them with drug addictions. The police later deduced that Berdella wasn't quite so generous as he claimed in his relationships with these young men. They believe he was exploiting them for sex. By now, Berdella was pretty open about his sexuality and most people he knew were aware that he was gay.

Berdella murdered for the first time in 1984. His victims were all young men that he had gained the trust of and then isolated. The murders were very sadistic - even for a serial killer. Berdella would drug and restrain the victims and then basically torture them for as long as they could survive. The victims were raped, cut, given electric shocks, and he would even inject them with cleaning fluids in the neck so they couldn't scream. Berdella would often the break the bones of the victims' hands with an iron bar so that they couldn't put up a struggle.

Berdella claimed to have been influenced by the 1965 film The Collector (which adapted a novel by John Fowles) - where an alienated young man is obsessed by a female student and makes her a captive in his cellar. He wanted his victims to become compliant and trust him. However, most of them died from torture long before they got anywhere near this stage. Berdella's disturbing activities came to an end in 1988 when a male prostitute named Christopher Bryson, after days of torture, managed to escape from Berdella's home and run across the street (in a dog collar). He found some police and told them what had happened.

The badly injured Bryson was taken to hospital and the police eventually obtained permission to search Berdella's home. They found that he had an elaborate torture room but the worst was yet to come. They also found human skulls and a human head. There was a chainsaw covered in human blood and various body parts. The police also found photographs Berdella had taken of his victims in various stages of torture. Berdella had also written detailed diaries of his torture methods.

Berdella was sentenced to life imprisonment without the possibility of parole. He had to do a plea bargain to avoid the death penalty. This involved a full confession in order to help identify all of his victims. Berdella was the worst sort of serial killer in that he was more interested in torture than death. He would keep his victims alive as long as he could before he killed them or they died.

Berdella never seemed to express much remorse for his terrible crimes. When he was in prison he complained that the authorities withheld his medication for high blood pressure. He died of a heart attack in 1992 at the age of 43. It's safe to say that no one had much sympathy when they heard he had died. When the judge at Berdella's trial heard the killer had died in prison, he is reported to have smiled and said - "Couldn't have happened to a nicer guy."

Javed Iqbal was born in Lahore, Pakistan, in 1956. Iqbal is regarded to be the worst serial killer in the history of Pakistan. His is a strange and disturbing story. Javed Iqbal came from a solid family and went to college. He then started his own business and lived in a villa that his family owned. He was though gay and in the 1990s he was arrested by the police in Lahore for an alleged act of sodomy. Iqbal was greatly angered by this - specifically because it caused his mother much shame and distress. Iqbal blamed his arrest for his mother's mental and physical problems and somewhat premature death.

As his 'revenge', Iqbal decided to start murdering local boys so that their mothers would have to grieve like his mother did. This all sounds completely bonkers (and it IS clearly bonkers) but in the frazzled and disturbed mind of Javed Iqbal it presumably had some sort of twisted logic. He claimed to have killed around one hundred boys (ages from six to sixteen) by means of strangulation. He then dissected the bodies and disposed of the remains in acid.

A lot of his victims were orphans and homeless street kids. After he put the remains in vats of acid he would dump the containers in the river. In 1999, Iqbal sent a letter to the chief of the local newspaper in which he confessed to these murders. When the police were called in they naturally searched his house and found evidence of human bloodstains. There were also photographs of his victims and some body parts still festering in acid. Four teenage boys who lived with Iqbal were arrested on suspicion on being accomplices. One of these alleged accomplices died in police custody.

The judge at the trial decided that Iqbal should die in the same manner that he killed his victims. "You will be strangled to death in front of the parents whose children you killed," said the judge. "Your body will then be cut into 100 pieces and put in acid, the same way you killed the children." However, Pakistan's interior minister Moinudeen Haide said such a sentence was not permitted. "We are signatories to the Human Rights Commission. Such punishments are not allowed." It was all academic anyway. Before the execution could be carried out, Javed Iqbal hung himself in his prison cell in 2001. He was 45 and his bizarre and evil life was over.

Randy Kraft was born in Long Beach, California in 1945. Kraft killed dozens of men from 1973 to 1982. His targets were hitchhikers - who he would give drugs and alcohol and then often strangle. Kraft was known as The Scorecard Killer because he kept a tally of his victims in the fashion of a scoresheet. The odd thing about Kraft is that he was intelligent and worked in computers. Those that had known him at school said he was the least likely person to be a serial killer one could imagine. Kraft was a bright student who had hopes of becoming a politician one day. He was a Republican at first but then became a Democrat.

Kraft deduced that he was gay from from a fairly young age. In 1966 he was charged with lewd conduct after making a sexual advance to an undercover police officer. Kraft joined the US Air Force as a young man but was discharged when his sexuality became apparent. In those less enlightened times it was all but impossible to serve in the armed forces if people thought you were gay. Randy Kraft began his killing spree in 1971. All of the victims were young males under the age of 35. Many were Marines who Kraft picked up on the road and then drugged.

Kraft would often torture the victims and then abuse the bodies before strangling them with a belt. Like many serial killers he had a fetish for dominating an incapacitated or dead person. He burned the eyes of one body with a lighter and once threw a human head off a jetty. Kraft, tragically, seemed to get away with his activities for a long time. He was sometimes capable of stopping for a while and he also killed his victims in some different areas. It was probably somewhat complicated at times for the authorities to categorically connect all of his murders and definitively say they were done by one person.

One of Kraft's victims was tied to a tree and had leaves and dirt shoved down his throat. Kraft raped the victim and then cut his genitals off. Tragically, Kraft was spoken to by the police in 1975 and some detectives wanted to press charges against him but the police decided they simply didn't have enough evidence and so Kraft was released without charge. Kraft was eventually arrested several years later in 1983 after two two traffic cops noticed him driving in an erratic fashion. When they pulled him up he had a dead body in the car with him. The police later searched Kraft's car and possessions and found a folder which contained dozens of explicit pictures of young men who appeared to be either sedated or dead.

On May 12, 1989, Kraft was found guilty of sixteen counts of murder, one count of sodomy, and one count of emasculation. The police believed that Kraft killed around sixty-seven men in total. Kraft was sentenced to death but remains alive and on Death Row to this day. He never confessed to any of the murders. "I can't imagine doing these things in scientific experiments on a dead person, much less someone alive," said the judge at Kraft's trial. "If anyone ever deserved the death penalty, he's got it coming."

TRIAL

Dennis Nilsen's October 1983 at the Old Bailey trial lasted ten days. In the run up to his trial, Dennis Nilsen fired his solicitor Ronald Moss and declared that he would defend himself. Had this happened, Nilsen wouldn't have been the first serial killer to defend himself. Ted Bundy and Rodney Alcala are among the serial killers who have defended themselves at murder trials. Bundy and Alcala, despite having high IQs (especially Alcala), were both absolutely hopeless at this. They both came across as creepy and cold in court. There is no question that the same fate would have befallen Nilsen. Nilsen was sensibly told by the magistrate that defending himself would be a ridiculous and stupid course of action. Nilsen, on hearing this, re-applied for legal aid and allowed Moss to come back.

Dennis Nilsen was 37 years-old when his trial took place. He pleaded not guilty to all charges at his trial on the grounds of diminished responsibility. If his diminished responsibility plea had been successful, Nilsen would probably have ended up in Broadmoor. Dennis Nilsen's defence team went for a diminished responsibility defence and tried to depict him as mentally abnormal. This was obviously an attempt to have the charges reduced to manslaughter. Nilsen's police interviews were so detailed and rational though that it was easy for the prosecution to argue that Dennis Nilsen was perfectly aware of what he had done. Dennis Nilsen's plea of diminished responsibility was completely contradicted by the calm and article fashion in which he conducted his lengthy police interviews.

Dennis Nilsen was very reluctant to consent to a plea of diminished responsibility. Despite his situation, his vanity made it difficult for him to accept that there was anything 'diminished' about his personality. One of Dennis Nilsen's fears after his arrest was that he might be sent to a mental asylum. He was very fearful of being termed 'mad' or insane. This would explain why he tried to resist entering a plea of diminished responsibility. Many felt that the Dennis Nilsen trial indicated that definitions of sanity and diminished responsibility needed to be looked at again. While it was true that Nilsen was aware of what he had done and seemed 'normal' in person it would be ludicrous all the same to call him sane given his crimes. There is clearly nothing sane at all about watching television with a dead body next to you or strangling people and boiling their heads.

Dennis Nilsen was a complete tabula rasa in court. He didn't show any emotion at all. Dennis Nilsen said that his professional training in the police and army was why he seemed unemotional in police interviews and during his trial. Nilsen claimed that he had been taught to remain calm and concise in stressful situations. At the trial, the Daily Mirror's court reporter said that Dennis Nilsen looked more like a bank clerk on his day off than a notorious killer. During the trial, the Daily Express court reporter, on a similar note, wrote that there was something of the 'primness of a fussy clerk' about Dennis Nilsen. All of Dennis Nilsen's police interviews were read out in court during his trial. This took a total of four hours.

The victims of Nilsen who escaped and were able to give evidence at the trial did have their evidence contradicted and vigorously challenged by the defence but the mere fact that they were court testifying that Nilsen had attacked them was damaging enough in itself. The trial displayed photographs of the murder scenes but the jury were spared anything too grisly or disturbing. Some of the relatives of Nilsen's victims attended the trial. The police had advised against this because they knew it would obviously be a distressing experience. Several newspapers were in contempt of court around the time of Nilsen's trial because they published articles about the case before a verdict had been reached. Dennis Nilsen was very crafty during his trial. He often pointed out inconsistencies in prosecution witness statements to his lawyer.

The prosecution were unfailingly polite to Dennis Nilsen in

court. This was an interesting tactic that proved to be effective. The defence team at the trial had to rely on psychiatric analysis in their (doomed) attempt to prove that Dennis Nilsen was unaware of what he had done. Alan Green, who led the prosecution at the trial, called Dennis Nilsen a "jolly good actor" who knew exactly what he had done (despite Nilsen's diminished responsibly plea). At the trial, the prosecution agreed that the murders nor the victims were homosexual by nature. This meant that, sensibly, the sexuality of Nilsen and his victims was not a factor in the case. The sexuality of Dennis Nilsen and the victims was not really a factor in the trial evidence. This was a case about murder. It didn't really matter if people were gay or not.

The trial established that Dennis Nilsen had a strange desire for self-destruction. He knew he was peering over the abyss but he couldn't seem to stop himself. Alan Green mostly relied on Nilsen's police interviews when handling the case for the prosecution. Paul Nobbs (Dennis Nilsen said he decided not kill Paul Nobbs because there was no longer any room under his floorboards to store more victims) and Carl Stotter, who testified against Nilsen in court, were both so nervous that they had to be asked to speak up by the judge. Carl Stotter literally had no money whatsoever at the time of the trial so the police paid his taxi fare so that he could come to court and be a witness.

When he gave evidence during the trial, the reliability of Douglas Stewart as a witness was attacked by the defence because it came to light that he had sold the story of his encounter with Dennis Nilsen to the Daily Mirror. Toshimitsu Ozawa, a Japanese student who escaped Nilsen at Cranley Gardens, said in court through a statement - "He had a normal expression on his face, but he was looking at me. He didn't say anything to me. I wasn't unnerved by what he was doing as I thought he was joking. He put the tie round my neck and started to pull the two ends together." Ozawa fortunately managed to run from the house.

At the trial, a man who once stayed at Nilsen's flat for eight days at Christmas said that Dennis Nilsen had no Christmas decorations and no Christmas cards. There was no Christmas dinner and no mention of Christmas at all from Nilsen. At the trial, it was reported that, for New Year's Eve in 1981, Dennis Nilsen invited his neighbours to his flat but they all said they had made other plans. This compounded his sense of being an outcast in society.

The trial suggested that Dennis Nilsen had a split personality. During the trial it was reported that Dennis Nilsen had an imaginary friend that he referred to as the 'professor'. Other killers have said something similar. The killer Joseph James DeAngelo said he called his urge to kill 'Jerry'. It was like a demon on his shoulder. Ted Bundy called the part of him that murdered the 'entity'. Dennis Radar called his urge to kill 'Factor X'. This could be an explanation for why Nilsen was sometimes overheard consulting with the 'professor'.

During the trial, a letter written by Nilsen was read out in court in which he said - 'Could it be a case of the individual exaltation in beating the system and a need to beat and confound it time and time again? It amazes me that I have no tears for these victims. I have no tears for myself or those bereaved by my action.' Dr Paul Bowden, a psychiatrist for the prosecution, said though that Nilsen displayed emotion to him at Brixton Prison when they discussed one of the murders. "Tears filled his eyes and he was about to start crying, and he spoke about never being able to show his feelings, then he got up and walked out."

Members of the jury at Dennis Nilsen's trial were especially distressed when they heard details of how the remains of his victims often attracted maggots. One of the skulls of Nilsen's victims was used as evidence in the trial. The big cooking pot that Nilsen used to boil skulls, hands, and feet, was also brought to his trial to be used as evidence. Dennis Nilsen's cooking pot was later put on display in the Crime Museum at Scotland Yard. Dennis Nilsen's bath also ended up in Scotland

Yard's Crime Museum.

The psychiatrist Dr Patrick Gallwey, a defence witness at the trial, said that Nilsen suffered from 'Borderline False Self As If Pseudo-Normal Narcissistic Personality Disorder'. The jury (understandably) had no idea what he was talking about. Gallwey's evidence was weakened by his confusing use of psychiatrist jargon. Dr Patrick Gallwey said of Nilsen - "He was behaving like a machine. He is a cold-blooded killer who is not responsible for his acts." At the trial, a psychiatrist for the prosecution named Dr Paul Bowden said that he didn't believe there was any medical excuse or explanation for Nilsen's behaviour. He had interviewed Nilsen and simply found him to be a cold and manipulative man. Dr Paul Bowden argued at the trial that Dennis Nilsen had a mental abnormality but not a mental disorder.

At Nilsen's trial, Alan Green, summing up for the prosecution, told the jury - "The defence are saying that he couldn't really help it, and the prosecution are saying: 'Oh, yes, he could.' He was free to choose – and he did choose – who to leave alone and who to kill and who to reprieve, and greater power hath no man than this, say the prosecution. He is a plausible fellow, a person who is able to bluff his way out of many a situation."

Alan Green said that Nilsen killed for pleasure. Green said that Nilsen might have had an abnormal mind but he was not suffering from a known medical condition and knew exactly what he was doing. The High Court described Nilsen's offences as 'as grave and depraved as it is possible to imagine'. Dr Pat Gallwey, Nilsen's defence psychologist at the trial, said that although Dennis Nilsen was quite intelligent he had no emotions whatsoever. Nilsen was aware that he had killed people but he did not emotionally understand the gravity of what he had done. This is naturally a common trait in serial killers.

Dr Patrick Gallwey said of Dennis Nilsen - "He has an area of his life in which he behaves perfectly normally. Alongside that he is having to keep at bay these disturbances which are part and parcel of a schizoid and paranoid personality. He is under constant strain between the normal area and the disturbed area. Although they are in equilibrium, it is potentially a very, very unstable one." Dr James MacKeith said at the trial that Nilsen had a severe personality disorder. He noted that there was a curious aspect to Nilsen in that that he realised he was now famous but didn't seem to understand he was notorious. Dr James MacKeith said that Nilsen was grandiose and had a big ego.

The jury were spared having to look at grisly photographs of the scene police officers found in Nilsen's flat at his trial. Instead, it was described to them in detail. When Nilsen's defence team tried to argue for diminished responsibility, the prosecution were able to use a quote that Nilsen had given the police during his interviews. Nilsen had told the police - "At the precise moment of the act [of murder], I believe I am right in doing the act."

On November the 4th, 1983, a majority verdict found Dennis Nilsen guilty of six counts of murder and one of attempted murder. The jury took over twelve hours to reach a verdict at Nilsen's trial. There were two dissenters (on the issue of diminished responsibility and everything except the attempted murder of Paul Nobbs) on the jury at Nilsen's trial so the judge accepted a majority verdict.

Dennis Nilsen was sentenced to life imprisonment with a recommendation that he serve a minimum of 25 years. There was zero chance that he would ever be released and he never was. Mr Justice Croom-Johnson, in sentencing Dennis Nilsen at the trial, said - "Dennis Andrew Nilsen, on the verdicts of the jury on the murder counts, there is only one sentence which it is possible for me to pass. I have had to consider whether I should make any recommendation in this case on the minimum period which in my view you should serve before any consideration is given to your release. It is a rare thing to be done but in the present case, I do make such a recommendation, that it be 25 years."

In his summing up at the end of the evidence in Dennis Nilsen's trial, the judge told the jury that "a mind can be evil without being abnormal." Believe it or not, the majority of serial killers are usually deemed to be sane when subjected to tests. The Daily Express reported that Nilsen had a 'smug look of satisfaction' when he was found guilty at his trial. The judge said that even if Nilsen had received a manslaughter verdict on the grounds of diminished responsibility he still would have received the same sentence because his condition was essentially untreatable.

In his 2001 essay, Brain Damage, Nilsen wrote - 'At 4.25pm on Friday the 4th of November 1983 the State through the agency of the Judicial system made its pronouncement on me. The anonymous jury, having gained its thrills and shocks from this theatre of the absurd had finally, by a majority of 10-2, agreed with the judge's and prosecution's view of me and my past actions. The media would take up the clarion call of me as 'Evil beyond belief'. The flashbulbs flashed and the wolves howled and in the universal public consciousness I joined the ranks of the damned alongside Crippen, Haigh, Brady, Hindley, and Sutcliffe.'

Although he never appealed his sentence, private notes by Dennis Nilsen revealed that he did at least consider an appeal when he was upgraded to full life tariff in the early 1990s. The whole life order (formerly a whole life tariff) is a court order whereby a prisoner who is being sentenced to life imprisonment is ordered to serve that sentence without any possibility of parole or conditional release. Even if Nilsen had appealed his sentence it would have been fairly pointless. It's hard to imagine any court or Home Secretary would have allowed him to have parole or a lesser sentence. What politician would have ever put themselves in a position where they had to explain why they'd released Dennis Nilsen?

After he was found guilty of murder, Dennis Nilsen said he

went back to prison and was allowed to watch some television. He watched the television in a blank haze as it slowly began to sink in that he would never be a free man again for the rest of his life. Of his life sentence in prison, Nilsen wrote - 'We are dead men locked in a tomb; the living dead, privileged by selective animation. We are required to be neither seen nor heard.'

THE DROWNING BOY

Nilsen had to complete a sex offender course in prison. He said the course taught him nothing he didn't already know. The arrest of Dennis Nilsen and his trial made headlines around the world. Nilsen had some parallels to the American serial killer Edmund Kemper in his attitude to capture. Nilsen and Kemper both seemed relieved to have been caught and talked openly about their crimes. Kemper and Nilsen are probably the two serial killers who made the biggest effort to diagnose themselves - although Kemper always felt more concise and intelligent than Nilsen when doing this. Kemper was a lot like Nilsen in that he had done dreadful things (including necrophilia) but didn't seem insane in the slightest.

The gay community were never happy with the way the Dennis Nilsen case was reported in the tabloids. The tabloids often gave one the impression that the gay community was rife with dangerous murderous men preying on teenagers. Dennis Nilsen was obviously a tragic aberration though and no more representative of gay people than someone like Peter Sutcliffe was of heterosexual people. Dennis Nilsen said that as a gay man who lived through the sixties and seventies he already felt like a criminal even before he was arrested for murder.

In the 1980s, Nilsen took to wearing a pink triangle on his prison uniform as a symbol of Gay Liberation. During the AIDS crisis in the 1980s, Dennis Nilsen even wrote to the Gay Times arguing that condoms should be handed out to inmates in prison to make any sexual activity safer. It was rather strange for Nilsen to depict himself as a champion of gay people when he had killed a dozen or so gay men!

There have, since Nilsen, been other killers who prey on the gay community. Nilsen was never consulted though on any of these cases - even though he might have been able to provide some insight. In the United States for example, police detectives consulted the incarcerated Ted Bundy when they were trying to catch the Green River Killer (Gary Ridgeway). The two killers had similar methods so they thought it was worth a shot talking to Bundy. The police could (and probably should) have caught Dennis Nilsen much earlier. If they had taken the complaints made against him more seriously then lives could have been saved. *

Dennis Nilsen was attacked a few times in prison. This would be one explanation for why he was moved around a lot. It seems logical to presume that Nilsen was shuttled around prisons for his own safety. It is also believed that because he was such a pain in the neck (with his constant complaints and legal threats) that no one prison could put up with him for too long. Nilsen suffered a nasty prison attack in 1983 and received 90 stitches. The man who attack Nilsen in prison in 1983 was a 21 year-old named Albert Moffat. Moffat slashed Nilsen in the face with a razor. One can see a long scar on Nilsen's left cheek in photographs from this period. The attack happened at Wormwood Scrubs.

Albert Moffat was judged to have acted in self-defence when he attacked Nilsen. Moffat said that Nilsen had made sexual advances and that he was merely protecting himself. Albert Moffat said of his attack on Nilsen - "I have no remorse about what I did. I'm sorry it wasn't 189 stitches he got instead of 89 because the man is a monster. I would have no hesitation in doing it again. I didn't do him any harm. Nilsen is a coward when it comes to face-to-face conflict. He can only kill people when they are drunk or drugged. There should be an inquiry into why he was let loose inside among young men. He is clearly insane and should never be released. Forget about the recommended 25 years."

After the attack by Albert Moffat, Dennis Nilsen was moved from Wormwood Scrubs to Parkhurst. Albert Moffat said that Nilsen had lunged at him with some sort of metal object. "I wasn't going to stand there and let him start chopping me to pieces," he said at the trial for the attack. Albert Moffat was due for release when he attacked Dennis Nilsen. He was held in custody until a trial for the attack could take place. Nilsen never seemed though to become a regular target for other prisoners. Someone who killed children would have been in much more danger than Nilsen. Nilsen killed a fourteen year-old but, as we have noted, this was only revealed in 2006.

Photographs of Nilsen in custody in 1983 show that he grew a mustache at one point. He didn't make it permanent. In 1983, the Guardian reported that a psychiatrist said of Nilsen - "We can't classify him. We don't have the classifications for such a weirdo." The Guardian also reported in 1983 that one person who viewed Nilsen's old flat at Cranley Gardens pondered aloud whether it might now be haunted. A waxwork of Dennis Nilsen at Madame Tussauds was unveiled in 1984 - a year after his crimes were uncovered. The waxwork of Nilsen at Madame Tussauds was in the Chamber of Horrors alongside notorious figures like Jack the Ripper. The section where the waxwork of Dennis Nilsen at Madame Tussauds was placed also included instruments and recreations of various methods of execution.

Serial killers who are captured often fall into two categories. Those who insist they are innocent and those who seem to enjoy talking about crimes. Nilsen was definitely the latter. Dennis Nilsen later acquired a typewriter in his prison cell. He would spend hours clacking away on this old machine. Dennis Nilsen famously wrote an autobiography while in prison. Dennis Nilsen's autobiography was a two volume memoir originally entitled Dennis Nilsen: The History of a Drowning Boy. It was written in the late 1980s. The British High Court and Home Secretary ruled in 2003 that the book should never be published. The book would eventually see the light of day though in 2021.

Dennis Nilsen said that his motivation to write his autobiography was that - "I have spent almost nine years in a climate of long and detailed introspection, without counselling or therapy of any positive kind. Therefore it has fallen on me to prove the secret recesses of my personality in the hope that I may understand the engine of my actions and effect solutions to problems in a non-destructive way". The longest part of Nilsen's autobiography was the third section dealing with his time in prison. By 1996 he had a manuscript said to be 400 pages in length.

In his book, Nilsen likened himself to a dog that had never been patted. Dennis Nilsen also said he was amazed to discover how easy it was to kill someone without anyone noticing. Nilsen wrote of his crimes - 'I did it all for me. Purely selfish. I worshipped the art and the act of death, over and over. It's as simple as that. Afterwards it was all sexual confusion, symbolism, honouring the "fallen." I was honouring myself. I hated the decay and the dissection. There was no sadistic pleasure in the killing. I killed them as I would like to be killed myself, enjoying the extremity of the death act itself. If I did it to myself I could only experience it once. If I did it to others, I could experience the death act over and over again.'

Nilsen's introduction to Orientation in Me, the first volume of his autobiography, read - 'This short study is not a full autobiography. It is a narrative compilation including what I believe to be the salient features of my Sexual History. The only serious attempt to interpret my life was the book by Brian Masters, Killing for Company. However, my autobiography, 'History of a Drowning Boy' (written in 1988/89) has never been published and, thereby, my exposition of myself in full studied detail has not seen the light of day. Every author is entitled to his interpretation of a subject but one is not obliged to agree with his conclusions. I have spent almost nine years in a climate of long and detailed introspection, without counselling or therapy of any positive kind. Therefore it has fallen on me to prove the secret recesses of my personality in the hope that I may understand the engine of my actions and effect solutions to problems in a non-destructive way.

'In this short study I offer my own conclusions at the end. In measuring the spectrum of human conduct, none of us can, as yet, simplify man's infinitely varied behaviour into a set of definitive answers. All we can hope to do is gather and interpret as many of the common traits and features with a view to help us understand humanity better than ignorance and prejudice. I apologise in advance for the state of this first draft manuscript. I did no rough notes in longhand but put the recollections that came to mind straight from the mind onto this typewriter. As I was under the pressure of having to produce so much in such a short time (three weeks) and at moments when I was not engaged on other things. The entire text is replete with typing slips, errors and omissions due to the sheer speed of production. I have barely had time for anything other than a quick read over of what I have produced.

'It is not a full study because of the tight time factor but I trust it will be helpful in understanding the long road from childhood to the present day. I have tried not to replicate or repeat material I have produced in my Brixton prison journals of 1983. The narrative ends in 1985 because since then there has been practically no sexual element in my life. The second reason is that any man has a right to some recent privacy. Suffice to say that my sexuality today has in it no element of violence against other persons. I have not felt attracted to anyone sexually since I left Wakefield Prison in early April 1990. I hope this document will assist the reader in understanding the Orientation in my past life. This is comprehensive and I have held nothing, that springs to mind, back. I am willing to answer any questions not answered herein.'

Dennis Nilsen is far from the only serial killer to write an autobiography while in prison. Donald "Pee Wee" Gaskins, Ian Brady, Myra Hindley, and Danny Rollings, amongst others, also wrote autobiographies while in prison. Few of these books were ever published. The problem with the 'memoirs' of serial killers is that we don't know what is embellished or fictional. These books are rightly suppressed for the most part anyway. When he went to prison after his arrest, Nilsen would sometimes try to interest other inmates with a book of his poetry. One wouldn't imagine there were many takers. Nilsen's furious writing (poems, memoirs, essays, letters of complaint, pen pals etc) was clearly his way of dealing with the boredom of prison.

Dennis Nilsen said in a letter from prison that he did have remorse and wept privately for his victims. This was taken with a large pinch of salt. He never showed much sign of remorse or emotion in court or interviews. Though some killers have expressed remorse for their crimes, a number of experts doubt that serial killers are truly capable of this emotion. Nilsen's attempts to get his autobiography publish were incredibly arrogant and insensitive. If you were a relative of one of the victims, literally the last thing you'd want to see is a book come out where the killer writes in graphic detail about the crimes and rambles on pompously about his life. The autobiographical stuff that Nilsen wrote in prison was pretentious and obtuse. He was not a reliable narrator.

One of Dennis Nilsen's hobbies in prison was to compose music on a Casio keyboard. He apparently composed eighty pieces of music. Dennis Nilsen worked in the prison library translating books into Braille. Nilsen is believed to have transcribed 184 books into Braille while he was in prison. In letters written in prison, Nilsen boasted about staging a play behind bars as if he was some great undiscovered artist. Dennis Nilsen is said to have kept himself to himself in prison. He didn't mix much with other prisoners. It is said that Nilsen liked to read newspaper accounts of his case and crimes. He was amazed to become so famous - even if this was the worst sort of fame imaginable. Dennis Nilsen said prison was not an ordeal for him and that being in the British Army in the 1960s and 1970s was much tougher.

Nilsen was a subscriber to the satirical magazine Private Eye and always had copies in his prison cell. He was largely well behaved but did have his strops. Dennis Nilsen is alleged to have once thrown a bucket of urine at a prison officer - this incident apparently happened in Brixton Prison. Nilsen was prisoner B62006 while in prison. People who interviewed Nilsen or mingled with him in prison say that they never felt uncomfortable in his presence. He never gave off any aura of danger. Although Nilsen is compared to Edmund Kemper (in that both were articulate and confessed to their crimes), the big difference is that Kemper gave himself up to the police. Nilsen did not - not until five minutes to midnight when the game was finally up.

It is often reported that Dennis Nilsen had a relationship with David Martin in prison. David Martin was a notorious criminal who allegedly carried out burglaries dressed in women's clothes. There is though scant evidence that Nilsen and Martin had that much contact at all in prison. Dennis Nilsen said that he had no interest in sexual prison encounters after 1990. There are few photographs of Nilsen in prison. One that does exist shows him smirking and posing in a vest. This might derive from the time when he was confined to his cell for refusing to wear a prison uniform.

It was rather pathetic that Nilsen seemed to enjoy his dark fame. He genuinely seemed to think he was a celebrity. When he was in prison, Dennis Nilsen later wrote to a penpal saying that he was more famous than David Beckham. "A thought has just hit me. What have I in common with David Beckham? Answer: We are both exhibits in Madame Tussaud's. Alas, like all sportsmen his star will fade in time and he will be melted down and replaced by some new sensation. Worse still, I guess, my infamy is destined to go on and on." Dennis Nilsen was said to throw a tantrum if any anyone pointed out that, for a notorious serial killer, he was surprisingly dull and ordinary in person. Nilsen hated the suggestion that he was ordinary or dull in the flesh.

A film was actually made about Dennis Nilsen in 1989 called Cold Light of Day. However, the film is so low-budget and amateurish that it was quickly forgotten. Cold Light of Day was directed by Fhiona-Louise and features Bob Flag as Nilsen (called Jordan March in the film although it is clearly based on Nilsen). The film is a rather grim experience. It shows Nilsen/March strangling people and boiling heads. The

Allslightsceserved blog wrote of Cold Light of Day - 'Cold Light of Day, despite the involvement as producer of horror stalwart Richard Driscoll - writer/director of such reviled work as The Comic (1985) and Kannibal (2001) - is not a piece of exploitative kitsch.

'Admittedly it does deviate from the facts of the Nilsen case; only three murders are committed here and the otherwise effective Bob Flag is slightly too old for the role, given Nilsen was only 37 at the time of his arrest. But its portrayal of a lonely, desolate world of dingy pubs and greasy spoons, where people in need of comfort are driven to extraordinary lengths, is a deeply an unsettling one. We watch Jordan interacting with his fellow tenants and even taking steps to ensure an elderly neighbour receives proper care and support. He's the kind of ordinary, seemingly decent bloke who might live down your street, and that true horror sometimes lurks behind the most banal exteriors.'

Time Out was less charitable in their view of Cold Light of Day - 'A very lightly disguised drama-doc on Cranley Gardens serial killer Denis Nielsen (here named Jordan March), who disposed of at least 13 young loners and losers, presumably based on Brian Masters' fine account in his book Killing for Company. March (Flag) looks like Roy Orbison wearing a Black-and-White Minstrels wig; the film has the lighting and look of an Andy Warhol home movie - heads cut off, lots of static shots of men on sofas - and a soundtrack composed of deep breathing, the pounding of a demolition ball, and church bells. Little light is thrown by March in the police interrogations on the reasons for his actions ('I didn't mean to. It just happened') or by the film itself. We see March as a boy, presumably traumatised by witnessing the death of his grandfather. Mostly we see strangulations, heads being boiled, viscera being scooped, hands being hacked. Risibility vies with banality; result, objectionability.'

BFI wrote of Cold Light of Day - 'Fhiona-Louise's Cold Light of Day, released six years after Nilsen's sentencing, is a curious, chilling film. The protagonist, Jorden March, is clearly based on Nilsen, from his appearance to the nature of his crimes. Unlike Des, it depicts a couple of the murder victims, but does not establish their characters. They are essentially in the film so we can watch them be strangled, see their naked corpses on the floor and witness the disposal of their bodies. Although the film is not without merit, it's not immediately clear why it was made. It's too loose with the facts for true crime fanatics. A shocking appearance of a severed head notwithstanding, it's not gory enough for horror fans. It is not particularly interested in political or social commentary.'

Plans to make feature films about the Moors Murders (believe it or not the famous American film director William Friedkin was once attached to a Moors Murders film) and the Yorkshire Ripper were shelved in the end because they were deemed too controversial. You will probably never see a studio feature film about Nilsen for the same reason. Cold Light of Day hardly counts because it was an 'underground' effort that didn't get a proper release. The film Cold Light of Day was very controversial when it came out and considered to be in very poor taste. Dennis Nilsen once joked that if they made a film about him the cast would have to be listed in order of disappearance.

Dennis Nilsen was shuttled around eight different prisons in the end. In 1991, for his own safety, Nilsen was moved to Full Sutton prison. While he was in prison, Nilsen complained that most gay prisoners were still in the closet. Nilsen felt like he was a rarity in that he didn't hide his sexuality. After his death, letters from Nilsen came to light in which he said that while he was at HMP Whitemoor he had a relationship with a fellow prisoner named Jimmy. Nilsen complains in the letters that the authorities separated the pair and destroyed the letters that he tried to give Jimmy.

Nilsen spent some time in a Vulnerable Prisoner Unit while he was behind bars. He said this was a terrible experience because these units were used to house child sex offenders. As such, these units were a target for other prisoners - who would do things like arrange to have razor blades put in the meals. Nilsen actually had to work in a wood mill when he was sent to the prison on the Isle of Wight in the early 1990s. This came as a rather nasty shock to him. He just wanted to sit in his cell writing.

* 'For a murderer so prolific he has been branded Britain's second worse serial killer, who was able to murder up to 15 men between 1978 and 1983, it is remarkable that the crimes of Dennis Nilsen was only discovered after his neighbours complained about their blocked drains,' wrote Crime Investigation. 'Despite the fact Nilsen was known to police, his arrest and confession only came after a plumber, who was called in to investigate the pipes near Nilsen's Muswell Hill home, discovered human remains Nilsen had tried to flush. Why he wasn't caught earlier? Maybe it has to do with the victims he preyed upon and the police's attitude towards them.

'For years, Nilsen targeted the vulnerable: young men and boys (some as young as 14) who were part of groups that police have historically been accused of ignoring: most were gay, many were homeless and runaways and some were involved in sex work. When allegations against Nilsen surfaced, they were seemingly disregarded and dismissed by police, who wrote them off as 'gay crimes'. Can police homophobia account for the reason Nilsen wasn't caught sooner? It seems so.

'In 1980, Douglas Stewart woke up in Nilsen's home to find Nilsen attempting to strangle him. Stewart managed to escape and alert the police, showing them the marks on his neck. Yet despite that, police dismissed it as a 'homosexual lover's tiff'. Carol Stottor also reported Nilsen to the police, after Nilsen suffocated him while he was staying at Nilsen's home. (Nilsen later resuscitated him and allowed him to leave.) But Stottor wasn't contacted again until Nilsen had already been arrested —following a confession.

Innate homophobia runs through this case. Paul Nobbs testified that he never reported his own encounter with Nilsen to police for fear of his sexuality being discovered. And Nilsen himself was a victim of homophobia: homosexuality was still illegal when he was growing up in Scotland and he later left the army because of the homophobia he encountered there.

'It's not a complaint unique to this case. The same allegations of police prejudice, which have in turn led to inaction or negligence, occurs in other cases that affect the LGBTQ+ community, the killers benefiting from the fact that their victims are part of a stigmatised group. It's not a complaint unique to this case. The same allegations of police prejudice, which have in turn led to inaction or negligence, occurs in other cases that affect the LGBTQ+ community, the killers benefiting from the fact that their victims are part of a stigmatised group.

'One of Jeffrey Dahmer's victims, 14-year-old Konerak Sinthasomphone— who had been drugged and attacked by Dahmer, before managing to escape—was even returned to Dahmer by police, despite the fact he was cut, bleeding and naked. Dahmer was already on probation following a second-degree assault on a 13-year-old boy and had the bodies of other victims in his home when the police entered it. But police concluded it was a 'lover's quarrel', describing the then 31-year-old as Sinthasomphone's 'boyfriend' and laughing about the entire incident.

'Sinthasomphone was murdered soon after they had left. Police also knew of Bruce McArthur, the prolific killer behind the murders of men from Toronto's gay village between 2010 and 2017—the disappearances of whom the gay community had already accused police of not taking seriously—after he attacked a gay sex worker with a metal bar in 2002. Relations, in fact, were so bad between police and the LGBTQ+ community that uniformed officers were banned from Pride Toronto in 2017 and 2018. Police in Los Angeles faced similar accusations over the case of Ed Buck, who was able to murder

Black gay men for years without repercussion. His victims were often homeless and addicted to drugs. One victims' mother said she was treated by police like a criminal, accusing them of ignoring evidence, as well as the men who spoke out.

'The UK's police force also continues to be called out for its negligence when it comes to crimes affecting gay men. 'Gay Slayer' Colin Ireland murdered five men in three months before he was arrested. Despite similarities between the bodies and the fact that he met all of his victims at the same pub, police were slow to connect the deaths. Ireland even started leaving clues for the police at the scenes. His arrest came only after he turned himself in. Ireland's case was mentioned in a 2007 report that found that 'institutional homophobia' had hampered Scotland Yard's reactions to attacks and murders of gay, lesbian and trans people. A lack of knowledge, reliance on stereotypes and personal prejudice were quoted as being behind the failures.

'Though it noted progress had occurred since the 90s, when Ireland was operating, the same mistakes continue to be made, as was the case in 2014, with Grindr Killer Stephen Port. Despite the fact that they had been warned by the Met's LGBT independent advisory group that a serial killer was at work, police failed to connect the deaths of Port's victims, which were taken as suicides or drug overdoses. Similarly to Nilsen, Port was known to police for his involvement in the death of one of the men, Anthony Walgate. His computer had even been seized, but police failed to search it. If they had, they would have found disturbing online searches. Victims' families later sued for the homophobia they said stopped the police from connecting the victims' deaths and which led to more murders.

'As recently as last year, the BBC reported that prosecution by police for hate crimes was falling, despite the fact that the numbers of victims coming forward was on the rise, with victims quoted in the piece stating police had done little to investigate their cases. And gay officers within the force have also backed up the allegations of innate homophobia. So what can be done to ensure that police homophobia is tackled? There are no easy answers, especially when prejudice is so deep rooted—both in individuals and the force as a whole. Cases like Port's, though, highlight that the sexuality of LGBTQ+ victims continues to be taken into account in a way that isn't true of straight victims. While that continues, so will inequality in the justice system.'

DAHMER VERSUS NILSEN

In 1991, an American serial killer named Jeffrey Dahmer was captured in Milwaukee. Dennis Nilsen is to this day sometimes dubbed Britain's Jeffrey Dahmer - although Dahmer actually came after Nilsen. You might suggest that Dahmer WAS actually the American Dennis Nilsen - though with some qualifications. The story of Jeffrey Dahmer was, in some areas, even more grisly than the story of Dennis Nilsen. One would hardly think that was possible. What could be worse than Dennis Nilsen?

Jeffrey Dahmer ended up in an identical situation to Nilsen. They both ended up trapped in a top floor flat festooned with body parts that they couldn't dispose of. Like Nilsen, Dahmer was a gay serial killer who would murder young men he had lured back to his flat. Dahmer and Nilsen were also both in the armed forces as young men. Dahmer, like Nilsen, boiled the flesh and kept victim body parts in his home. The biggest difference between Dahmer and Nilsen is that Dahmer ate body parts of his victims. He was a cannibal.

Dennis Nilsen was once asked by Brian Masters if he had ever been tempted to eat his victims (like Jeffrey Dahmer did). He replied - "Oh, never, I'm strictly a bacon-and-eggs man." Dahmer and Nilsen both wanted to stop killing but neither was capable of this. Only capture would finally end the madness. Just as towns in Britain are often twinned with somewhere in Belgium or France you might say that Dennis Nilsen was twinned with Jeffrey Dahmer across the Atlantic. There were plainly a number of similarities between them.

Jeffrey Dahmer was born in Milwaukee in 1960. Relatives of Jeffrey Dahmer say that his personality seemed to suddenly change after he had hernia surgery at the age of six. Dahmer became very interested in taxidermy and decomposition and his chemist father taught him how to preserve animal bones. Dahmer was a very bright kid and had an IQ of 145 as an adult.

However, he developed a drinking problem at a young age - which seemed to blight whatever potential he had. Dahmer was also gay and so all of his future victims would be men that he had picked up or developed a friendship with. When he was growing-up, Jeffrey Dahmer once stole a mannequin from a store and kept it in his bedroom. He had a sexual fantasy where he dominated an inert lover. This fantasy was by no means uncommon when it came to serial killers.

Dahmer said he first had a fantasy about killing someone when he was in high school. He is believed to have killed for the first time when he was eighteen. Dahmer murdered a hitchhiker he had picked up by hitting him with a weight. Dahmer used acid to dissolve the body and crushed whatever bones were left with a hammer. After dropping out of university, Dahmer became a combat medic in the 8th Infantry Division and was stationed in West Germany. Two soldiers who served with Dahmer claimed that he sedated and raped them in Germany. Jeffrey Dahmer was eventually kicked out of the army for his drinking though. After he was discharged, Dahmer went home and worked in a chocolate factory before moving in with his grandmother. Dahmer began to pick up men and there were more incidents of him sedating and sexually assaulting victims.

In 1987, Jeffrey Dahmer woke up in a motel with the dead body of a man next to him. He somehow managed to get the body out of the motel using a suitcase and took it to his grandmother's home (where Dahmer lived) so that he could dissect the body and dispose of it. Soon after, Dahmer moved into an apartment and his killing spree began to spiral out of control. Jeffrey Dahmer said he tried to stop killing but it was a compulsion he just couldn't ignore. Jeffrey Dahmer's apartment was so eventually so full with victims and body parts that he put one body in the bath and had to shower over it. The apartment contained a plastic drum of acid where three human torsos were dissolving.

Jeffrey Dahmer poured acid into the head of a victim named

Konerak Sinthasomphone. Sinthasomphone escaped and wandered the streets in a daze. Tragically, some policemen who found Sinthasomphone then took him back to Dahmer's apartment after Dahmer told them Sinthasomphone was his intoxicated boyfriend. Dahmer was so crazy that he thought if he injected acid into a victim they would become a compliant slave for him. Dahmer would sedate his victims by giving them a drink that was laced with sleeping pills. Dahmer once drank the spiked drink he had laced for a victim by mistake. He passed out and when he woke up the victim had robbed him and left. Naturally, Dahmer didn't bother to report the crime. The 'thief' had no idea how lucky he had been that Dahmer gave him the wrong drink by mistake.

Dahmer is most famous for the fact that he would eat parts of his victims. Jeffrey Dahmer fried the body parts of his victims in a skillet before he ate them. Dahmer used a meat tenderizer to make human flesh more edible. During his police confession, Jeffrey Dahmer was asked if he ate human body parts plain. He replied that he ate them with salt & pepper and steak sauce.

Neighbours of Jeffrey Dahmer did complain about the smell coming from his apartment once. He apparently told them that his fridge broke and some food went bad. Dahmer had a tray at the bottom of his fridge to collect the blood that dripped down from body parts. Jeffrey Dahmer would sometimes make sandwiches for neighbours in his apartment building. It is therefore possible that his neighbours might have unwittingly eaten human flesh. Dahmer liked to paint human skulls because he thought this made them look fake and they would be less suspicious if discovered. He used formaldehyde to preserve body parts.

Jeffrey Dahmer was captured when a man named Tracy Edwards managed to escape the handcuffs Dahmer had put on him and go and fetch some police officers. Dahmer had two hands and human genitalia in his kettle when the police searched his apartment. This was merely the tip of the iceberg.

One of the police officers later described Dahmer's apartment as like entering a real life horror museum. It was very grim and disturbing. The police found a complete skeleton in Jeffry Dahmer's filing cabinet and three human heads in the fridge. Dahmer seemed relieved to have been caught and spent hours giving them a full confession.

In his confession, Jeffrey Dahmer said that when he cut up his victims he would remove his clothes and place the victim in a tub. He said he felt brief remorse for the victim but this did not last. Mostly, he felt excited. When he was captured, Jeffrey Dahmer told the police that he retained the skulls and bones of his victims because he wanted to use them to construct a place of meditation. Dahmer said that, circa 1983, he tried to use religion to fight off his desperate urge to kill. It obviously didn't work.

Dahmer was tried in Milwaukee for 15 counts of first-degree murder. The death penalty was not an option in the state so Dahmer was sentenced to life behind bars. He did some interviews while in prison. Despite the gruesome and unfathomable nature of his crimes, Dahmer seemed alarmingly normal and mundane in interviews. He was articulate and soft-spoken. Dahmer didn't serve much of his sentence in the end. In 1994, another prisoner (a convicted murderer named Christopher Scarver) attacked Dahmer and another inmate named Jesse Anderson with an iron bar after some sort of altercation. The attack was so violent that Dahmer later died in hospital. He was 34 years-old and the life of one of the most infamous serial killers in American history had ended.

Dennis Nilsen (who was plainly wrong about this) didn't actually believe that Jeffrey Dahmer was really a cannibal. "He is talking subconsciously. It's a kind of wishful thinking," said Nilsen. "What he really wants is spiritual ingestion, to take the essence of the person into himself and thereby feel bigger. It's almost a paternal thing, in an odd way." Nilsen, as he was with all serial killers, didn't seem comfortable when he was asked about Jeffrey Dahmer. It was like a threat to his identity in a sense - the fact that on the other side of the Atlantic was a man who had an almost identical MO and set of crimes (save for the cannibalism).

The emergence of Dahmer in 1991 made Dennis Nilsen seem (believe it or not) slightly less unique. Dahmer became more famous than Nilsen. Madame Tussauds might even have had to put their Dennis Nilsen waxwork away and replace it with one of Dahmer. How Dennis Nilsen must have hated that. It was uncanny though to note the similarities between Dahmer and Nilsen. Both of them were in the army. Both of them were big drinkers. Both of them picked their victims up in bars. Both of them were intelligent. Both of them were gay. Both of them wore glasses. And both were motivated by necrophilia. Nilsen and Dahmer both said exactly the same thing when they were captured. They both said that they killed their victims so they wouldn't leave. Dahmer and Nilsen were both terrified of being alone.

Dahmer and Nilsen both felt that an apartment full of dead bodies was preferable to an empty apartment. They enjoyed the company of dead people. And they both sexually abused the dead bodies of their victims. The absolutely bizarre and grim circumstances of Dahmer and Nilsen were almost identical when they were arrested. They were both living in small flats surrounded by death and decay. Dahmer was more creative than Nilsen with his use of acid but they were both in the same situation. Body parts all the place, stuffed in cupboards or drawers. The stench of death everywhere. Both Dahmer and Nilsen had to dismember their victims when decomposition made keeping the body as a 'toy' impossible

Psychopaths in Life wrote of Dennis Nilsen - 'It is this tendency for people to leave him, combined with a psychopathic desire on his part for power and control over others, that led to him preventing some guests from leaving by killing them and keeping their corpses. He would then keep the corpses in his flat, often for days, sometimes even conversing with them as if they were still alive. This represented an extreme and perverted need for control over others which is prevalent in all psychopaths to some degree. If he couldn't make them stay with him voluntarily, it is as if he would force them to stay with him by murdering them. However despite this need for control, his lack of emotional connection with his victims is apparent in the way he treated their bodies when he wanted rid of them, cutting them up like pieces of meat and keeping them in his apartment or else burying them in his garden. Once he no longer needed them them they were nothing to him, just objects to be disposed of.'

As we have noted, necrophilia is not rare at all in the most notorious true crime cases. It's a common theme in many serial killers. Gary Ridgway was born in 1949 in Salt Lake City, Utah. He is known as The Green River Killer and was convicted of 49 murders. The true kill count is almost certainly a lot higher than that figure. Ridgway, like many serial killers, targeted sex workers and teenage runaways and hitchhikers. Ridgway would usually strangle the victims and then sexually abuse the bodies - which he would leave in the woods and return to again. Gary Ridgway said he sometimes tried to bury victims as soon as he could because otherwise he was tormented by an insatiable urge to have sex with the corpses. Ted Bundy (by now captured) was consulted by the police when they were trying to solve the Green River Killer case. Bundy told the police that the killer probably returned to burial sites to visit the bodies of his victims. He was certainly right about that.

Jerry Brudos was a serial killer who murdered four women in Oregon from 1968 to 1969. Brudos was a rapist and necrophile who killed because he couldn't control his foot fetish. He sawed off the foot of one victim and put in the freezer. He would then often take the foot out of the freezer and put ladies shoes on it. Jerry Brudos cut off the breasts of one of his victims so he could make plastic moulds with it. Jerry Brudos actually got married. It was said that he liked his wife to do the housework naked wearing nothing but a pair of high heeled shoes. Jerry Brudos was thankfully captured quite quickly. He died in prison in 2006. His prison cell was said to be full of ladies shoe catalogues when he died.

The notorious graverobber Ed Gein was born in La Crosse County, Wisconsin, on August 27, 1906. He is not generally felt (in terms of statistics) to be a serial killer but he might well have been. Gein probably killed more people than he is officially credited with. Gein had an isolated life on the family farm but his mental health eroded after the death of his mother and brother. Gein's brother died in a mysterious accident involving fires on the farm. Many suspect Ed Gein of killing his brother. Ed Gein never got over the death of his mother. He was a childlike man who was fond of lurid paperbacks and comics that featured stories about cannibals and Nazis. In 1957, Plainfield hardware store owner Bernice Worden vanished. The police deduced from cash register receipts that Ed Gein had been one of the last visitors to the store so they went to his farm. At the farm they found the body of Worden decapitated and hung up like a deer. It turned out too that Ed Gein had been digging up bodies from the local cemetery and making masks, furniture, and skin suits from them.

At Gein's farm, the police also found the head of a woman named Mary Hogan who had been missing for three years. Gein used female genitalia in some of the bric-a-brac around his home. He'd also fashioned some skulls into serving bowls. When the police searched Ed Gein's house they found his kitchen full of maggots. They could not fathom how anyone could live in such squalor. The police found one room in Gein's farmhouse untouched and free of ghoulish graveyard bric-a-brac. His mother's bedroom - save for dust - was exactly how she had left it when she died. You might say this was pure Norman Bates. Gein was one of the first killers to gain national attention in America. His crimes were so bizarre that a morbid fascination with the case was unavoidable. Gein was arrested and sent to a prison hospital. Ed Gein's farm burned down after his arrest (it was said to be accident but you never know).

The locals were very happy when this happened because they didn't want the farm to attract curious sightseers.

Patrick Wayne Kearney was born in East Los Angeles in 1939. He confessed to 35 murders but the true figure is most likely considerably higher. Kearney is sometimes known as The Trash Bag Killer in true crime biographies. This is because he would dismember his victims into trash bags and dump them by the side of the road or put them in the desert. He was not only a killer but a necrophile too. Kearney spent most of his spare time trawling the underbelly of the gay scene. His victims were mostly young men but he killed boys too. Kearney was only 5'5 tall and not the most physically imposing man. For this reason he used a gun and would shoot his victims dead while they were asleep or sitting in the car passenger seat next to him. He would then drive to a secluded spot and sexually abuse the body. Kearney said he would sometimes punch and kick the bodies of dead victims because he found this cathartic.

Thor Nis Christiansen was a Danish-American killer who murdered four young women in California from 1976 to 1979. Christiansen was also a necrophile. In fact, this is what had motivated the murders in the first place. He had been overwhelmed by dark fantasies of shooting a woman dead and then having sex with the body. John Christie was born in Yorkshire in 1899. Christie murdered at least eight people in London in the 1940s and 1950s - mostly by use of domestic gas. Once they were unconscious he would rape and then murder the victims. Christie is arguably not strictly a necrophile but he was close enough. He liked his victims to be inert and lifeless before he raped them. Dead or unconscious - it made no difference to Christie.

Earle Nelson was born in 1897 in San Francisco, California. He tends to be known as The Dark Strangler. Earle was the first prolific American serial killer of the 20th century (indeed for many years he thought to be the MOST prolific American serial killer - at least until the serial killer explosion of later years). Nelson's killing spree began in 1926. His modus operandi soon became clear. Nelson would dress him quite smartly and, Bible in hand, pretend to be a Christian traveller looking for a room to rent. His targets were middle-aged landladies. Once he had charmed the landlady sufficiently and got his foot inside the door (so to speak), Nelson would strangle them (sometimes with a chord) and then usually have sex with the body. He was - of course - a necrophile in addition to being a serial killer. He is credited with 22 murders but there are at least seven unsolved murders where he is considered to be a suspect.

Yoshio Kodaira was a Japanese serial killer who raped and murdered at least seven women from 1945 to 1946. Kodaira would lure the victims to rural spots under the guise of offering them employment. He was found to have a particular fondness for having sex with the victims after he had killed them. Reginald Oates is an American killer who killed four young boys within the span of two days in April 1968, in Baltimore, Maryland. Oates had sex with the bodies of the victims after their death. When he was captured he had body parts (including genitals) from the murdered victims in a bag. Oates was deemed too insane to stand trial and sent to the Clifton T. Perkins State Hospital in Jessup.

Serhiy Tkach was born in Russia in 1952. He tends to be known as The Pavlohrad Maniac. There are 37 confirmed victims of Tkach but he claims to have killed a hundred people. Believe it or not, Serhiy Tkach worked as a criminal investigator. Tkach targeted young girls (none older than eighteen) who he then raped and suffocated. There is evidence that Tkach was a necrophile as some of the victims were apparently sexually abused after death. Ted Bundy said that after he killed a woman, he would sometimes shampoo their hair so they had less of an odour. Bundy would have sex with the bodies until decomposition made this impossible. The victims were usually stored in the woods so that Bundy could go back and visit them.

Tsutomu Miyazaki was a killer active in the late eighties and early nineties. He has been described as the Japanese version of Albert Fish. His victims were all very young children (always female) and he would post the remains to the relatives as a means of taunting them. Miyazaki was fond of necrophilia and also once returned to one of the bodies weeks after the murder to cut off the feet. Tsutomu Miyazaki was captured when he tried to abduct two girls but was noticed and had to flee. The police arrived quickly enough to capture him before he could hide or get out of the area. Miyazaki was executed by hanging in 2008. The case of Tsutomu Miyazaki was very traumatic for the people of Japan.

'Necrophiles,' wrote psychologytoday, 'have increased likelihood to commit homicide before carrying out necrophilic acts, simply because diminished empathy and antisocial behaviour are characteristic of these disorders. There has also been suggestion that those who have committed necrophilia have suffered from depression and schizophrenia in the form of anthropophagy and vampirism. The need for an unrejecting partner is universal for most humans who desire an intimate relationship with another living human, as is the need to feel accepted. And so with necrophilia, it would be worth assessing all of the qualities people look for in a living person (using dating websites, and the ample pop psychology outlets), and seeing if those needs could be met with a deceased partner. A dead partner is not judgmental, there is no fear of needing to produce a reciprocal orgasm during sex, they cannot emotionally hurt anyone, they can be trusted, they do not answer back, there is no concern about offspring, and they can meet what is only a temporary need for sexual intimacy. The necrophiliac also has the luxury of creating, imagining, or fantasizing the corpse to be anything they want it to be.'

It is sometimes said that you don't get necrophile female serial killers like Dennis Nilsen or Jeffrey Dahmer but this isn't true at all. Piroska Jancsó Ladányi is a case in point. Piroska Jancsó Ladányi was born in the Hungarian town of Törökszentmiklós in 1934. She had a rough childhood and was abused by Red Army soldiers (Hungary was at this time an occupied puppet state of the Soviet Union). Piroska was said to be cruel to animals from a young age and is also alleged to have engaged in incest with her brother. It was a messed up start in life to say the least.

Piroska didn't have much schooling but she enjoyed reading novels and was said to be of above average intelligence. Like many serial killers she also had early convictions for theft. Her first victim was eleven year-old Marika Komáromi in 1953. Piroska isolated the child and then strangled her with chicken wire at a farmhouse. She then undressed the body and sexually abused the corpse. After she was satisfied, Piroska dragged the body outside with rope and hid it underneath some metal sheets. The other victims were killed in 1954. The next victim was a thirteen year-old girl named Hoppál. Piroska strangled the girl and then sexually abused the body. Piroska said she inserted a carrot into herself while she was doing this. Hoppál was then thrown into a well.

Irene Simon, who was seventeen, was the next victim. Piroska killed this girl because she was having a sexual relationship with her and didn't want anyone to find out. She decided the best solution to that worry would be to simply murder her lover. Irene Simon was strangled and thrown down a well. The next victim was thirteen year-old Marika Botos - who was on holiday with her grandmother. Once again, Piroska isolated the girl, lured her away, and strangled her before sexually abusing the corpse. Katalin Szőke, also thirteen, was the next victim. She was strangled with a belt strap before Piroska used the corpse to satiate her warped necrophile sexual desires.

Piroska took the clothes and belongings of the victims and sold them. By this time the deaths were starting to attract attention and a number of theories were juggled by the police. Soviet soldiers and gypsies were the main suspects. The exploits of Piroska were ended by a 21 year-old woman named István Balázsi. Piroska tried to strangle Balázsi but she escaped and fled to the police. The police investigation eventually led them to the well where Piroska had dumped her victims.

At first, Piroska tried to pretend that male accomplices had done the murders but this was a blatant lie. She even implicated a Soviet soldier. This made the investigation difficult for the police because they obviously didn't have much authority over the Red Army. Piroska eventually came clean though and offered a full confession. She admitted that the murders were sexually motivated and said she had always been attracted to girls.

Piroska claimed that her mother was aware of the murders (it is said that it was Piroska's mother who had the idea of selling the clothes of the victims for money) and so at the initial trial her mother got two years in prison while Piroska was sentenced to death. After public outcry, Piroska's mother got a new sentence where she was sentenced to death too! This was commuted to life in prison though. There was no such luck for Piroska. In 1954 she was killed by hanging in the courtyard of the Szolnok prison. The gates of the prison were opened that day so that members of the public could come in and watch the execution.

Guadalupe Martínez de Bejarano, a Mexican female serial killer, was also a necrophile. Guadalupe Martínez de Bejarano is often called Mexico's first female serial killer and is known as La Mujer Verdugo (The Executioner Woman). The life of Guadalupe Martínez de Bejarano before her crimes is rather vague and nothing much is known about her childhood and birth. We do know though that she got married at some point and had a child. Martínez would find victims by interviewing people in her home with a view to employing them as a servant. This was all a ruse though. She would instead enslave and torture them.

Martínez was a sadist with a sexual motivation for her crimes. It is often assumed that only male serial killers are motivated by sexual desires but women like Guadalupe Martínez de Bejarano illustrate that this is not the case at all. The victims were lulled into a false sense of security because Martínez seemed fairly normal at first glance and had quite a middle-class sort of background. Being trapped in the home of Martínez turned out to be a nightmare. Once she had restrained her victims she would sexually abuse them and whip them ferociously. Some were hung from the ceiling or burnt. The victims were all female so we can safely presume that Martínez was probably a closet lesbian.

Martínez would starve the victims after she had satiated her sick and sadistic desires. The first victim was a girl named Casimira Juárez in 1887. Martínez was actually convicted for this murder but (unbelievbably) only served a few years in prison. Her next victims were two sisters named Guadalupe and Crescencia Pineda in 1892. Neighbours of Martínez had by now started to notice that something strange was going on. There were a lot of dark whispers about her. The police took action after hearing these complaints and found the dead bodies of the Pineda sisters.

Martínez tried to blame the murders on her son Aurelio and said she was completely innocent. However, her son told the police that his mother was a kidnapper, sadist, and murderer who had carried out these murders herself. This did rather beg the question of why Aurelio hadn't saved the victims or told the police about his mother before now. As a consequence, although he had nothing to do with the murders, Aurelio received a prison sentence for not doing anything to stop them nor report his mother to the police.

As for Guadalupe Martínez de Bejarano, for the crime of torturing and murdering three young women, she was sentenced to ten years in prison. It felt like a ludicrously light sentence given the gravity of the crimes and there was much outrage in Mexico that she didn't get the death penalty. It was all moot in the end though as Guadalupe Martínez de Bejarano died in prison fairly soon into her sentence. One might say that prison was a worse punishment than the death penalty for Guadalupe Martínez de Bejarano because she had a pretty rough time in prison and was under constant threat of attack from other inmates because of the cruel and disturbing nature of her crimes.

Jane Toppan is another female killer who seemed to have a sexual fetish for dead bodies. Jane Toppan was born in Boston in 1854. She was known as The Angel of Death. Toppan murdered at least 31 people with lethal injections in her duties as a nurse. Her parents were Irish immigrants and life was not exactly plain sailing for Jane Toppan as a child. Her mother died of tuberculosis and Jane Toppan's father was said to be so crazy that he once tried to sew up one of his eyelids. Jane Toppan was a bright girl though and entered medical school in 1885.

She was known as Jolly Jane to her colleagues because she was always laughing and smiling. Everyone seemed to like her. She worked at Cambridge Hospital in Massachusetts and developed a fondness for working with patients who were sick or elderly. Jane Toppan first attracted mild suspicion in her medical duties because she was completely obsessed with autopsies. She was absolutely fascinated with death and loved going to the morgue. Jane Toppan used her patients at the hospital to experiment with the drugs morphine and atropine. She would vary the doses to see what reaction occurred in the patient. Naturally, she created bogus medical charts for her patients to disguise what she was actually doing.

Jane Toppan is said to have got a sexual thrill from her murders. She said she even climbed into bed with one patient she had just killed. In 1889, she worked at the Massachusetts General Hospital and continued to murder patients with overdoses. However, her murders were not just confined to the medical world. In 1895 she killed her landlord by poisoning and also murdered his wife. Jane Toppan then killed her sister Elizabeth with strychnine. You didn't have to be in hospital to be at risk from Jane Toppan. She would murder people anywhere given half a chance.

In 1901, Jane Toppan was hired as a private nurse to look after an elderly man named Alden Davis. You can probably guess what happened next. Yes, she murdered this man. But she didn't stop there. She also murdered his sister and two daughters. The relatives of the victims were understandably suspicious of Jane Toppan after these tragic and sudden deaths. They arranged for a medical test on the youngest daughter and the tests concluded the reason for death was poison. After she was taken into custody, Jane Toppan confessed to many murders.

Toppan told the police that she was perfectly sane and always knew exactly what she was doing. She said to the police - "That is my ambition, to have killed more people — more helpless people — than any man or woman who has ever lived." Toppan told the police that she experienced a thrill from having absolute power over patients and enjoyed taking them to the brink of death and then reviving them - and so on. Despite her claim that she was perfectly sane, it was clearly obvious that Jane Toppan was not sane in the least. Jane Toppan was so disturbed she had even poisoned herself once to appear ill and attract sympathy from a prospective boyfriend.

We will never know exactly how many people she actually killed. By any standards, Jane Toppan was completely ruthless. She once poisoned her best friend so that she could have her friend's job as a matron. Jane Toppan would kill literally anyone given the chance. As for explanations for why this woman became a compulsive killer, Jane Toppan was once jilted at the alter when she was supposed to get married. This is speculated to have been one of the sources of her anger and mental instability. "If I had been a married woman, I probably would not have killed all of those people," she said. "I would have had my husband, my children and my home to take up my mind." Jane Toppan was found not guilty of her crimes by reasons of insanity and committed for life in the Taunton Insane Hospital. She died in 1938 at the age of 84.

Our enduring fascination with serial killers stems from the fact that they are completely unfathomable and alien to us. We are constrained in our actions by compassion, guilt, remorse, empathy, and kindness. Most of us are very squeamish. Serial killers are not constrained by any of these normal human emotions. They rape, torture, kill, cut up (and sexually abuse) bodies, and commit the most gruesome acts as if it was the most natural thing in the world.

The banality of evil is a phrase that could have been invented purely for Nilsen. Court reporters at the trial were shocked at how dull and ordinary he was in the flesh. There is no denying though that we find killers like Dennis Nilsen and Jeffrey Dahmer darkly and morbidly fascinating. Nilsen's story is darker than any horror film you could ever hope to invent. It is as bizarre as anything Stephen King or Clive Barker could write. Dennis Nilsen once wrote that he was an ordinary man driven to extraordinary conclusions. Nilsen genuinely seemed to think he was 'honouring' his victims by caring for their dead bodies and performing sexual acts with them.

THE LONE WOLF

In 1992, Dennis Nilsen was interviewed in prison for the Central Television show Viewpoint. The Home Office tried to ban the interview from being broadcast but a judge ruled in Central's favour and it was transmitted in September 1992. The Central Television interview with Nilsen was filmed at HM Prison Albany on the Isle of Wight and conducted by the Clinical Psychologist Paul Britton. Despite causing a rumpus in the media, the show only actually featured four minutes of Nilsen talking. A few short clips of Nilsen was part of a wider documentary about killers. Nilsen seemed a bit heavier and in need of a haircut but this aside he didn't look that much different from the man sat in the Old Bailey back in 1983. Dennis Nilsen was appropriately sinister and commanding in the interview. He relished the chance to talk about his favourite subject - himself.

In the Central Television interview, Nilsen said there were twelve victims and that he'd lied to the police about killing fifteen people. Nilsen told the offscreen interviewer there is no blood when you cut up a body that has been dead for a while. By this time the blood had congealed. * You can see in the interview that Nilsen is clearly relishing the attention. He loves the fact that someone has come to talk to him and that he is going to be on television. Nilsen had a big ego and that ego must have taken a dent somewhat when he later saw how little he featured in the actual show. Nilsen did read the newspapers though and keep abreast of the television news. He would have derived some satisfaction from the fact that he was in the headlines again thanks to the controversy over his appearance on Central Television.

Dennis Nilsen would clearly have loved more chances to appear on television. He would liked to have been interviewed more. American killers seem to have the freedom (whether one agrees with this practice or not) to conduct prison interviews much more than their British counterparts. You can find prison interviews with everyone from Ted Bundy to Jeffrey Dahmer if you look. However, you'll never find a prison interview with Peter Sutcliffe or Ian Huntley. As for Nilsen, he only got a few minutes. American serial killers are interviewed much more than British ones. They are allowed to become celebrities. This was clearly a source of irritation to Nilsen. His ego would have loved the chance to appear on television all the time.

It is said that Dennis Nilsen was always fascinated if he saw a mention of himself on the news or in a newspaper. Criminologist Professor David Wilson said - "Nilsen is so self obsessed, so desperate for his opinion to be the only opinion that counts and matters that he finds it easier to relate to have a conversation with a dead young man who isn't capable of answering back." While he loved the thought of appearing on television, Nilsen wasn't quite so enthusiastic about books. He got many requests to add his insight or input into crime books but, Brian Masters aside, he had no great interest in this.

The reasons why Nilsen tended to avoid helping people with crime books could be condensed to two salient probabilities. The first is that Nilsen wanted to write his own story and, as it turned out, he was deluded enough to think that this book would be published without too much trouble. That obviously wasn't the case - as we'll see later. The other reason why Nilsen was wary of assisting with crime books is that he wasn't very happy with the book Brian Masters had written about him. Nilsen said of the Brian Masters book - 'He misses insightful clues in the first part of the narrative and in the second part I vanish into a muddled array of psychobabble. The human is never explained, or answered.' Nilsen clearly thought that he could do a much better job of telling his own story.

In 1994, Dennis Nilsen telephoned Brian Masters from prison to say he didn't want to talk to him anymore. Masters was at the Garrick Club in London. When he heard that Dennis Nilsen was on the phone he went into a panic for a second because he thought Nilsen might have escaped from prison!

Brian Masters believes that Dennis Nilsen broke off contact because he (Masters) compared him to Jeffry Dahmer. While he seemed to take satisfaction in his infamy, Dennis Nilsen did not like to be compared to other serial killers.

Dennis Nilsen liked to write poetry and campaigned in prison to get his poetry published. In a strange quirk of fate, Nilsen had dealings with a probation officer in Wakefield Prison named Simon Armitage. Armitage later became the poet laureate. Of his time as a probation officer at Wakefield Prison, Simon Armitage said - "I didn't enjoy my time in the prisons. Dennis Nilsen was in Wakefield Prison when I was there, so I was face to face with someone who had done terrible, terrible things in a tiny little room."

As you might expect, the poetry of Dennis Nilsen was pretty bizarre. One of his poems was all about condoms. A pen pal of Dennis Nilsen described Nilsen's prison poetry in the following way - "Nilsen wrote his poems like lectures. He liked to throw in long words, however they didn't always make sense. He came across as arrogant." Dennis Nilsen referred to modern society as 'metropolitania' in his poems. Most serial killers are completely detached from reality. This was certainly the case with Dennis Nilsen. When he was in prison he (preposterously, in light of the fact that he was a serial killer serving a life sentence!) seemed genuinely baffled that his poems, books, and music were not allowed to be released to the outside world.

Serial killers tend to be narcissistic personalities and you could certainly put Dennis Nilsen into this category. He loved talking about himself and adopted a pompous and pretentious style of writing in his letters and autobiographical notes. In letters written from prison, Nilsen described himself as a 'viable' human being who had been forced into the role of 'lone wolf' by society. Dennis Nilsen once had two budgerigars in his prison cell. They were named Tweetles and Hamish. Those who corresponded with Dennis Nilsen when he was in prison said that he was obsessed with conspiracy theories.

Nilsen never really found it that difficult to adapt to prison. He was used to a regimented sort of routine after the army and it wasn't as if he'd given up an awful lot by being incarcerated. By the time of his arrest he was estranged from family and had few friends left. He was living in a dismal flat and didn't have much of a life beyond going to work. Nilsen was clearly one of those killers who actually wanted to stop killing. He was perfectly willing to accept a life behind bars if this is what it took. In his respect Nilsen reminded many true crime authors of Ed Kemper - an American serial killer who was also a necrophile like Nilsen.

Kemper was born under a full moon in Burbank, California, in 1948. Kemper's childhood (and indeed his entire life) was doomed thanks to his dysfunctional relationship with his mother. Kemper was devastated when his parents divorced and he was left with his mother. Kemper loved his father but hated his mother. His mother would constantly verbally abuse him and act as if he was a danger to her other children. This verbal abuse and lack of love clearly took its toll on the mental health of Kemper. He was eventually sent to live with his grandparents on a ranch but he didn't like them anymore than he liked his mother.

Edward Kemper killed his grandparents in 1964 when he was only fifteen years old. He was declared paranoid schizophrenic and sent to the Atascadero State Hospital. He shot and stabbed his grandmother and then calmly waited for his grandfather to get home so he could shoot him dead. Because he killed when he was still a child, Kemper is sometimes assumed to be the inspiration for Michael Myers in the Halloween horror films.

Kemper was released from the Atascadero State Hospital when he was 21. One of the reasons for this was that the staff liked him. They even allowed Kemper to became an unofficial part of the staff and test new patients with them. Kemper had an IQ of 145 and was very intelligent and articulate. They believed

Kemper was cured and no danger to anyone. This would obviously prove to be a tragic mistake.

The Atascadero State Hospital appraisal of Kemper read - 'If I were to see this patient without having any history available or getting any history from him, I would think that we're dealing with a very well adjusted young man who had initiative, intelligence and who was free of any psychiatric illnesses. It is my opinion that he has made a very excellent response to the years of treatment and rehabilitation and I would see no psychiatric reason to consider him to be of any danger to himself or to any member of society ... [and] since it may allow him more freedom as an adult to develop his potential, I would consider it reasonable to have a permanent expunction of his juvenile records.'

Kemper tried to join the police when he was released. Kemper used to hang out in a bar where police officers would drink. He was friendly with them and they knew him well. As a consequence, he was the last person they suspected when murders began to abound in the area. Kemper worked for the Highway Department but was still dominated by his mother - much to his irritation. However, he finally got a sense of freedom when compensation from a motorbike accident allowed him to buy a car. It had not gone unnoticed by Kemper that this part of California was full of female hitchhikers. Kemper said he picked up over 150 hitchhikers without harming them in the slightest before he started killing. Kemper said that whenever he saw a pretty girl one part of him wanted to go on a date with her and the other part of him wondered what her head would look like on a stick.

Kemper said one of the tricks he used to persuade female hitchhikers to get in his car was to pointedly look at his watch and make it seem like he was in a hurry. This made the victims feel like he was just a normal person in a rush to get to work. Kemper was 6'9 tall and weighed something approaching 300 pounds. His victims (some of whom were teenage girls) had little chance of fighting back. Kemper had began to carry a bag with handcuffs, knives, and plastic bags in his car. He would kill the hitchhikers by any means possible (hands, knife, gun) and then have sex with the bodies. Usually he would decapitate the victim after he was finished. Kemper said he called his urge to kill Little Zapples. Most of these murders took place in 1972 and 1973. His youngest victim was fifteen. Kemper said that when he killed and abused the body he pretended the victim was his mother.

On April 20, 1973, Kemper killed his mother with a hammer. Kemper cut out the tongue and larynx of his mother and put it in the waste disposal. He also used her decapitated head as a dartboard. Kemper then invited her friend Sally Hallett over to the house and decapitated her too. After he murdered his mother, Edward Kemper said that further murders would have no point. This was a rather chilling comment because it implied that Kemper felt his previous murders DID have a point. He decided to turn himself in. "The original purpose was gone," said Kemper. "It wasn't serving any physical or real or emotional purpose. It was just a pure waste of time. Emotionally, I couldn't handle it much longer. Toward the end there, I started feeling the folly of the whole damn thing, and at the point of near exhaustion, near collapse, I just said to hell with it and called it all off."

The police hung up on Edward Kemper when he made his first telephone confession because they thought it was a prank. He was eventually sentenced to life in prison. Nilsen, like Kemper, seemed to reach a point where he just wanted to be released from the madness of his circumstances. He'd had enough. Nilsen and Kemper had a self-awareness that many serial killers lack. Neither of them pretended to be innocent and neither of them had any desire to get out of prison.

Dennis Nilsen read The Guardian in prison and in his autobiographical writing said that he was a fan of the films of Stanley Kubrick. Dennis Nilsen claimed in prison that he was in correspondence with an actor and ballet dancer. Nilsen had a disdain for psychiatrists in prison because he believed that only he could understand himself. Dennis Nilsen's autobiographical output in prison contradicted itself over time or perhaps displayed a change of view. After he was arrested he once wrote that he shed no tears for the relatives of his victims. In later writing he seemed to modify this and say he was sorry for what he had done to the families of those he killed.

Any notion of future parole for Dennis Nilsen was ended by the (then) Home Secretary Michael Howard in 1994. Howard replaced Nilsen's sentence with one of whole-life order. A whole-life - or so-called "life means life" - order means the criminal is in prison for the rest of their life without ever becoming eligible for parole. The prison reformer Lord Longford, who was always (much to the annoyance of the media and most of the British public) trying to get Myra Hindley released, was one of Dennis Nilsen's few visitors in prison. Longford said that Nilsen had an 'excellent sense of humour' and was redeemable.

In 1996, Lord Longford said of Dennis Nilsen - "There is no question of him coming out for many years. He has been forbidden to have his music published outside the prison even for charitable purposes. That case bears directly on the Unstarred Question. Why should Dennis Nilsen not be able to have his music published outside the prison, even for charitable purposes and when there is no question of personal profit? He has been told--I believe that this is true of other prisoners in Whitemoor also--that in future he must not have both a typewriter and a keyboard in his cell. He has to choose one or the other. The man has done terrible things, but he is a creative man. He has written an essay on how he became a murderer, which has been published by Ruth Rendell in an anthology on murder."

Dennis Nilsen asked Lord Longford to stop visiting him in the end because Longford had strong religious views about homosexuality. Lord Longford said that Dennis Nilsen told him he had been gay since the age of seven. Nilsen was not the only notorious killer to get cheesed off with Lord Longford in the end. Myra Hindley also told Longford to stop visiting her. Brian Masters did not agree with the views of Lord Longford. "He (Nilsen) is being duly punished by society for what he did, which he knows perfectly well was wrong." Brian Masters said that Dennis Nilsen was mad in his soul. "He can make a cup of coffee and eat a slice of toast with the head of somebody bubbling a few inches away. If madness is anything, that is it." Brian Masters said he was in contact with Dennis Nilsen for about ten years before their communication ended.

In 1998, Dennis Nilsen wrote - 'I don't remember that much about the outside world having for the past 15 years had little exposure to its influences.' In 1999, Nilsen wrote once again that he had no desire to be released from prison. He did though constantly gripe about conditions in prison. In 1999, the Daily Star claimed that Dennis Nilsen might have secretly corresponded with Ian Brady. In his writing, Dennis Nilsen had once castigated the relatives of the Moors Murder victims by saying they offered nothing but hate and spite. This was an indescribably cruel and horrible thing to say. It illustrated the lack of humanity at the core of Dennis Nilsen.

In Inside Time, the newspaper for prisoners and detainees, someone who spent time in prison with Dennis Nilsen said Nilsen used to cheat at Scrabble all the time. Nilsen is also said to have played the piano in prison. The greatest punishment for Nilsen after his arrest was that he was sort of forgotten for a while. ** He wasn't allowed to be interviewed and later British killers like Ian Huntley, Harold Shipman and Fred West became more famous than him. Dennis Nilsen's 'fame' was definitely negated by the likes of Fred West, Ian Huntley and Harold Shipman. Were it not for these three notorious killers then Nilsen would have been more prominent and famous.

* In 1999 a man named Simon Charles in Nottingham was inspired by Dennis Nilsen when he killed his housemate

Grenville Carter. Simon Charles had read about how Nilsen dissected bodies in his flat and eventually disposed of the evidence. Charles, a man with a history of violence, had throttled his friend and chopped him up using just a Stanley knife and junior hacksaw — simply because he irritated him. He had read how Nilsen cut up his victims' bodies to dispose of them. Detectives said Charles remembered how Nilsen once talked how little blood there was when dismembering a body. Simon Charles cut his victim up into twelve separate pieces and then dumped the remains in a cemetery.

** It was only really the acclaimed ITV drama Des in 2020 that made Nilsen big news again and activated new curiosity in his life - but by the time this drama was broadcast Nilsen was dead. As we'll see later, the fact that Nilsen was dead came as something of a relief to the cast and crew.

EPIC NOBODY

In 2001, Dennis Nilsen tried to instigate legal action at Whitemoor Prison because he was not allowed access to uncensored gay nude magazines. Nilsen's legal battle concerning 'gay porn' was basically about the fact that Nilsen had complained that gay magazines were censored and had pages torn out when they reached him in prison. Nilsen thought this was an unfair double standard because other prisoners (who were obviously straight and not gay) didn't have their 'porn' magazines like Razzle and Escort censored.

Nilsen's legal counsel argued in court - "The fact of imprisonment does not eradicate one's sexuality. To deny the claimant expression of his sexuality because it is of a homosexual nature is cruel and made more so by the fact that he will never have the opportunity, so long as this stance is maintained, to have access to materials which enable him to express his sexuality." Though he wasn't a violent prisoner, Nilsen was a constant thorn in the side of prison authorities with his petty complaints and legal actions.

Nilsen's autobiographical prison writing about his childhood was dreadfully self-pitying and pathetic. Many people have had worse childhoods than Nilsen without becoming serial killers. In his letters from prison, Nilsen always tried to be self-deprecating. He felt sorry for himself but tried to hide this with bleak humour. Nilsen wrote tens of thousands of words in an attempt to self diagnose himself. The condensed version is that he was a misfit who found dead bodies attractive. Nilsen continued to try and get his autobiography published from behind bars but the authorities once again managed to block this memoir in 2003.

'Serial killer Dennis Nilsen will not be allowed to appeal against a High Court ruling stopping him from completing his autobiography,' reported the BBC. 'Nilsen's plea for a judicial review was rejected last month. Mr Justice Maurice Kay rejected an argument by Nilsen's lawyers for the case to be heard in the appeal courts. Nilsen had been trying to retrieve his partially-completed manuscript from prison authorities. He was battling to overturn the refusals of Home Secretary David Blunkett and the governor of Full Sutton Prison, near York, to return it. His lawyer Alison Foster QC had argued that the Court of Appeal should now consider his case because there had been no recorded precedents relating to freedom of expression under European human rights laws. The book, entitled Nilsen: History of a Drowning Man, was intercepted by staff at Full Sutton in 2001.

'They refused to return it unless they could make sure it contained nothing objectionable under a Prison Service law on prisoner communications. In his ruling last month, the judge said the secretary of state was "entitled to have regard to the likely effect of publication on members of the public, including survivors and the families of victims of Mr Nilsen's serial offences". He added: "I am unimpressed by the suggestion that anyone can choose not to read whatever may be published." Nilsen, 57, admitted killing 15 young men at his north London home and was jailed for life in 1983. He was sentenced with a recommendation that he serve a minimum of 25 years for six counts of murder and two of attempted murder. He was later made the subject of a "whole life" tariff.'

Dennis Nilsen eventually went to the European Court of Justice in his doomed attempts to get his autobiography published. The Daily Record calculated in 2011 that Nilsen's legal battles to get his book published had cost British taxpayers over £60,000. Nilsen hadn't lost the dogged and pedantic qualities that served him so well as a Union Rep and (briefly) police officer. He took pride in the fact that he could still be a rebel and pain in the neck. The poet Peter Paul Hartnett was one of the few people with a copy of the Nilsen autobiography. Hartnet corresponded with Nilsen for ten years.

Dennis Nilsen said that drugs were rife in prison. He said that people threw them over the walls for prisoners to pick up. In 2005 the tabloids reported that Dennis Nilsen had boasted of getting drunk and high in prison thanks to 'liver crippling hooch' and cannabis. The story of Nilsen boasting about his easy supply of drink and drugs in prison was classic tabloid fodder. You'd think going to prison was like a Club 18-30 holiday if you only read the tabloids. Nilsen said he wrote large tracts of his memoir while he was drunk or stoned (which hardly promised to make it a more credible document).

Dennis Nilsen kept up with current affairs in prison and complained about the Gulf Wars to pen pals. His humanitarian and socialist credentials were naturally rather hollow and laughable after his awful crimes. Nilsen was said to take an interest in new crime cases. In one of his letters he mentioned Ian Huntley. Letters that Nilsen wrote from prison indicated that he sometimes watched True Crime documentaries on television. Nilsen took a particular interest in the late nineties rumpus over Mary Bell (who killed two little boys in 1968 when she was eleven) contributing to a book about her life by Gitta Sereny. Mary Bell was released in 1980 and completely rehabilitated. Though he would never admit to it, perhaps Nilsen felt some envy at the fact that Mary Bell had been 'saved' while he hadn't.

Dennis Nilsen said he read around 25 books a year while in prison. Nilsen said that among the books he read in prison were Toast by Nigel Slater, The Lovely Bones by Alice Sebold, In Cold Blood by Truman Capote, and I Don't Want To Fight by Lulu. Those who knew Dennis Nilsen in prison said he was quite fond of quoting Jung. Letters that Nilsen wrote in prison revealed that he had a particular dislike for the TV shows Coronation Street and Big Brother.

When he was in prison Nilsen once tried to block a play at the Edinburgh Fringe that was loosely based on his life. He was desperate to maintain control over his dark 'legend' - even though this was essentially impossible. Criminal psychologist David Wilson said that Dennis Nilsen used to send him

Christmas cards from prison. Wilson said that Dennis Nilsen had no sense of humour about anything. "Dennis Nilsen wouldn't know a joke if it hit him in the nose. They (serial killers) just don't get humour." Nilsen continued to write furiously and in 2009 finished a new 8,000 autobiographical piece which he titled Epic Nobody. Dennis Nilsen wrote in prison that he was (in his own opinion) not inherently evil - though the relatives of his victims would probably beg to differ.

In 2013, Google shut down a blog which had been posting Dennis Nilsen's so far unpublished autobiography. The family of Billy Sutherland, one of Nilsen's victims, was the main voice in the protests. Billy's brother Seaton said - "This man is a monster and he should not be allowed a voice. This is attempting to glorify what he did, and it was the right decision to stop his autobiography ever being published. It is disgraceful that reputable sites are being used to get round the ban and someone should do something to pull the plug on this before it goes any further."

One of the few entries by Nilsen that made it onto the blog read - 'For the most part mine was a female dominated world. Mother, grandmother, aunt. I vaguely remember my grandfather when he was not away at sea as a fisherman. I remember him as a tall, quiet, powerful figure who took an interest in me. He would take me out on long walks over the sand dunes and golf links. It would seem that he had no real interest in my older half-brother or my younger sister. On the dunes at the far end of the bay, near the stream flowing into the sea, there was a concrete pill box, built as part of the sea defences against a possible Nazi invasion during World War II, which had been over for about four and a half years. He would take me into the dark slit-windowed pill box and take down my short pants and hold my penis and tell me to urinate. I must have been about four years old at the time.

'Tired by the long (to a child) journey I would invariably fall asleep and be carried home in my grandfather's arms. My conscious memory is of his strength and a feeling of comfort and security. These were my only real, one to one, personable physical contact with someone who took a beneficial interest in me. He may have been a tepid paedophile but I do not remember him as threatening or oppressive, unless the traumas of some unpalatable truth or event is still locked up in the sub-conscious. These days of granddad were of short duration because he died at sea, aged sixty-two, of a heart attack in October 1951. Then began my first encounter with the fact and mystery of 'Death'. I remember being carried under my mother's arm into the room where he lay encoffined and on display for all visitors. He looked asleep with his John Lennon-type spectacles and dressed, bizarrely, in white with his bare feet sticking out at the bottom. The rough weather-beaten skin of his face gave the impression that he needed a shave. I did not know how to react or what to think.

'After this brief viewing I was whisked back to bed in the other room. Apparently my older brother and, perhaps, younger sister were both subjected to it. He had been 'laid out' in the room in which I was born, slept and lived in. Thereafter he disappeared from my life leaving behind the stark memory of the uncertain fact of his disappearance. I was told that he was 'in heaven' but I knew not where that was. However it dawned on me that he was locked inside a box and buried six feet under the ground. If this – death – could happen to him, so tall and strong, then I feared that this could easily happen to me. I was shocked by the idea of death. The grown-ups had said that granddad had 'gone to a better place' and it horrified me that it seemed they were saying that, in many respects, what happened to him, and his fate entombed underground, was a good thing. As he lay there in his box that day, I was puzzled that he was ignoring me as if he had deserted me. I hoped that he would see me later 'when he was better'.'

While there was undoubtedly a morbid curiosity about Dennis Nilsen's book, the extracts on the blog didn't suggest that a literary masterpiece was gathering dust in a drawer somewhere. There was obviously a question of taste when it came to publishing Nilsen's book. There is an argument that people like Dennis Nilsen are probably best forgotten (obviously this author doesn't agree with that view though people are entitled to have that opinion). If you were one of the relatives of his victims would you really want Nilsen's book to be released? Probably not in most cases you would imagine. Dennis Nilsen said he desired forgiveness from the relatives of his victims. This was clearly an unrealistic desire.

As we have noted, the greatest punishment for Dennis Nilsen was to prevent him from being interviewed or publishing anything. He hated to think that he had been forgotten. That's the point of prison. You make someone anonymous and lock them away. It doesn't matter how famous or notorious they were on the outside. In prison they simply become another prisoner. Dennis Nilsen didn't find prison tough but he did find it dull and his ego seemed to yearn for an unlikely limelight in the form of prison interviews and publishing books and music. Nilsen must have known deep down that this was all unlikely to happen. Maybe he just wanted something to battle against to keep himself occupied.

EPILOGUE

Estate agents who try to sell the two flats where Dennis Nilsen used to live are obliged to warn prospective buyers about the dark history of the properties. Dennis Nilsen's last home at Flat 23D Cranley Gardens, Muswell Hill, was put on the market to buy for around £250,000 in 2013. In 2016, The Sun reported that a couple had purchased Dennis Nilsen's old flat at Melrose Avenue for £493,000 and turned it into their 'dream home'. The couple said they were not bothered by the dark history of the property and didn't dwell on that. The garden, where Nilsen burned the remains of his victims, was now used by the couple to grow vegetables.

People in the area today where Nilsen had his two notorious flats still encounter 'serial killer' sightseers asking for directions to Melrose Avenue and Cranley Gardens. People are still curious to see the places where this awful crimes took place. You might say that the house at Cranley Gardens where Nilsen had his flat is sort of like the Muswell Hill version of Norman Bates' house in Pyscho. The Jobcentre where Nilsen worked in Denmark Street is now a branch of the Fernadez and Wells cafe chain. The dark aura left by Dennis Nilsen has faded and in some cases been completely forgotten or erased.

A few years before he died, Nilsen supposedly contributed to a horror novel by someone named Matthew Malekos. Matthew Malekos is an ex-psychiatric nurse who corresponded with Nilsen and had obviously tried to come up with some way to make money from this connection. The novel that Malekos wrote with Nilsen was called The Most Toys. Nilsen offered a pretentious introduction to the book. The most interesting thing about Nilsen's introduction is that he said he should have telephoned the police and turned himself in after killing his first victim. Sadly, it was a bit late now. Nilsen used the introduction to repeat his view that he was addicted to the 'ritual' of killing. This gave him an emotional connection that he could find no other way. In this, Nilsen was much like any other serial killer.

In one of his last prison letters, Nilsen complained about the price of washing powder. These trivial matters were all he had left to discuss. In a later letter from prison, Nilsen seemed to complain about the fact that academics were never allowed to visit him. He hated the fact that he been largely forgotten in prison and had no outlet to make his views known - or simply waffle on about himself to a captive audience. Nilsen described philosophy and history as two of his main interests in one of his last letters from prison. Nilsen also described himself as an Atheist in his correspondence.

When he was nearly 70, Nilsen wrote a letter from prison in which he said he was in good health and not on any medication. In another late letter from prison, Dennis Nilsen said he was against Scottish Independence. Nilsen wrote that, although he was Scottish, he was also proud of his service in the British Army and proud of being British. The fact that Dennis Nilsen was detached from reality was illustrated near the end of his life when he wrote that his army record was something he was proud of and proved that he was a worthwhile person. Preposterously, he somehow seemed to believe this mitigated his status as an evil serial killer! In one of his last letters, Nilsen mentioned the EU membership referendum but didn't say if he was in favour of leave or remain.

Dennis Nilsen died in 2018 at the age of 72. He was at HMP Full Sutton in East Yorkshire when he fell ill. Dennis Nilsen died in York hospital. Nilsen died of a ruptured abdominal aortic aneurysm. It was widely reported that Dennis Nilsen was in great pain when he died because he refused to comply with medical treatment. After his death, a report at Hull Prison (where Nilsen spent his last months) said that Nilsen never talked to the staff and had no close friends or associates in prison.

The BBC reported that Nilsen '... underwent an operation but later suffered a blood clot. Nilsen's inquest at Hull Coroner's Court heard he spent his final hours lying in his own filth as he suffered a ruptured abdominal aortic aneurysm. His medical cause of death was given as a pulmonary embolism and retroperitoneal haemorrhage, linked to the ruptured aneurysm. A report from the Prisons and Probation Ombudsman stated that Nilsen had been left deteriorating for two and a half hours after rejecting the opportunity to be seen for longer in the healthcare wing on the morning of 10 May last year. But it also stated that the treatment he initially received in prison was "commensurate with that which he would have received in the community.'

The official verdict from the authorities was that Nilsen died of natural causes. When Dennis Nilsen died, it was reported in the media that the Ministry of Justice paid £3,300 for him to have a private funeral and cremation. Dennis Nilsen's ashes were given to his 'next of kin'. Not much much else is known other than that. It is not known if any relations of Nilsen accepted his ashes. There have been many instances where the family of a serial killer have refused to accept the ashes after the killer has died.

Carl Stooter's sister said she shed no tears when she heard that Nilsen had died painfully. "When I read that he died in excruciating pain, I thought 'Good'. It's strange because Carl never once said he hated Nilsen, but what he did hate was the fact that Nilsen ended up having a much better life in prison than Carl ever did." A councillor from Fraserburgh expressed some public relief at the news that Nilsen had died. He hoped that this unfortunate and infamous link to their town might now be forgotten.

After his death, Dennis Nilsen's spectacles were given to a woman named Andrea Kubinova in the Czech Republic. Kubinova was Nilsen's penpal and visited him in prison. "He came across as a nice person," she said. "I know it's odd in the context, but yeah he was." Andrea Kubinova said that Dennis Nilsen told her he had no visitors in prison and that his surviving family had all disowned him. Andrea Kubinova said that when she met Dennis Nilsen in prison he was unrecognisable from the Dennis Nilsen of 1983. His hair was white and he was a rather hunched and frail figure.

Kubinova said that Dennis Nilsen had a great love of cheese & onion crisps and was fond of using the Oscar Wilde quote - The only worse than being talked about is NOT being talked about. In letters to Andrea Kubinova from prison, Dennis Nilsen said that he loved to watch Dad's Army. He described it as perfect comfort television. Andrea Kubinova said that Dennis Nilsen told her that his favourite food in prison was a fried egg sandwich. Andrea Kubinova also said that Dennis Nilsen told her that he dried his washing in prison on the radiator pipes. The letters painted a picture of a lonely old man living a tedious life behind bars.

There was a fresh wave of interest in Dennis Nilsen in 2020 when the ITV drama Des was broadcast. David Tennant played Nilsen in this miniseries. Luke Neal, who wrote the drama, said - "We were never going to show the murders, simply because the only person who knows what happened that night is unfortunately Dennis Nilsen, and he is the most unreliable narrator. He is a pathological liar. He is a narcissist, he is a psychopath. So we didn't want to trust him. So we wanted to tell another story, of the two men who tried to understand him, in very different ways. One tried to understand how he did it – and what he did – and the other one just trying to understand why he did it."

Luke Neal said that the Dennis Nilsen case was a terrible indictment of society. "I was also interested in what it says about our society that 15 people can go missing and nobody really notices. What kind of society allows someone like Dennis Nilsen to flourish for five years?" When they made the ITV drama Des, they couldn't speak to DCI Jay (who arrested Nilsen) because he sadly died a few weeks before the TV people were due to get in contact with him.

David Tennant said if Dennis Nilsen had been alive he probably would have gone to see him as part of research for the ITV drama Des. David Tennant said that in his research for Des he found Dennis Nilsen to be a boring person. It was true. Nilsen was genuinely dull in real life. It was only the grotesque things he did that made anyone interested in him. David Tennant said he was relieved that Dennis Nilsen died before the drama Des was broadcast because he believed Nilsen would probably have derived some pleasure at being the centre of attention again. It's hard to disagree with David Tennant's view that Nilsen would have enjoyed all the attention of featuring in an ITV drama.

ITV received a smattering of complaints about Des but not too many. The drama was fairly restrained and respectful. It didn't feature Nilsen strangling people and chopping up bodies or anything like that. British film and television is much more reticent to depict real serial killers on the screen than their counterparts in America. There have, for example, been six films made about Ted Bundy.

The 1989 film Cold Light of Day was given a Blu-Ray DVD release late in 2020. One might suspect this was to cash-in on the success of the ITV drama Des but the range of extras and interviews on Cold Light of Day suggests it had been in the planning for a while. For those that are interested in Cold of Light of day now that it has a proper DVD release, the film has a rating of 5.3 on IMDB. Let the buyer beware is the general view.

Dennis Nilsen still lingers on like a nightmarish folk memory. Poppy Z Brite's novel Exquisite Corpse is inspired by the grisly case of Dennis Nilsen. A company called Kulturmeister produced some serial killer playing cards or Top Trumps. Dennis Nilsen features and has a 'maniac rating' of three stars. He tends to be dubbed The Company Killer in such things.

There is a lot of weird serial killer 'memorabilia' floating around. Stuff concerning Dennis Nilsen is quite rare though.

An ebay user once tried to sell a short hand-typed letter by Dennis Nilsen for £700. The ebay user had his account removed as ebay have now banned the sale of serial killer 'collectibles'. A short letter typed by Dennis Nilsen is valued at $150 on a crime collectible website. A band called Macabre wrote a song about Nilsen called You're Dying to Be with Me. It was on their 2003 album Murder Metal. A website called TeePublic.Com sells Dennis Nilsen 'retro serial killer' t-shirts and tops. This seems rather tasteless to say the least.

At the start of 2021, Dennis Nilsen's long threatened 'memoir' History of a Drowning Boy was finally postumously published - all 368 pages. According to the blurb - 'Dennis Nilsen was one of Britain's most notorious serial killers, jailed for life in 1983 after the murders of 12 men and the attempted murders of many more. Seven years after his conviction, Nilsen began to write his autobiography and over a period of 18 years he typed 6,000 pages of introspection, reflection, comment and explanation.

'History of a Drowning Boy - taken exclusively from these astonishing writings - uncovers, for the first time, the motives behind the murders, and delivers a clear understanding of how such horrific events could have happened, tracing the origins back to early childhood. In another first, it provides an insight into his 35 years inside the maximum-security prison system including his everyday life on the wings; his interactions with the authorities and other notorious prisoners; and his artistic endeavours of music, writing and drama. It also reveals the truth behind many of the myths surrounding Dennis Nilsen, as reported in the media.

'Nilsen was determined to have his memoir published but to his frustration, the Home Office blocked publication during his lifetime. He died in 2018, entrusting the manuscript to his closest friend and it is now being published with the latter's permission. Any autobiography presents the writer's story from just one perspective - his own, and as such this record should be treated with some caution. An excellent foreword by criminologist Dr Mark Pettigrew offers some context to Nilsen's words, and this important work provides an extraordinary journey through the life of a remarkable and inadequate man.'

History of a Drowning Boy, strangely, seemed to pass by largely unnoticed apart from a few tabloid articles. Most people could be forgiven if they hadn't even noticed its publication. The book was compiled and edited from 6,000 pages of notes Nilsen left behind. Nilsen, with much time on his hands and a tremendous ego to boot, had naturally written a memoir to dwarf War and Peace in length. Most of the book concerns (in mind numbing and sometimes irrelevant detail) his early life in Scotland and then later devotes endless pages to his criticisms of the prison system. While prison reform is something we are probably all in favour of it is obviously somewhat difficult for the reader to dredge up endless sympathy for a serial killer complaining about the inadequacies of the prison system!

A lot of Nilsen's essays concerning his sexuality and fantasies had to be omitted from History of a Drowning Boy because they were deemed too extreme. As for the murders (which is unavoidably a reason why many people will read the book), Nilsen is somewhat restrained and clinical in writing about about these. He actually seems more interested in prison reform and his childhood in the book than he is with the fact that he's a serial killer. Perhaps the most interesting revelation in History of a Drowning Boy is that Nilsen seems to confess to previously unreported murders. He claims to have strangled two other victims who were never named or reported missing. This seems more than plausible. Nilsen probably wasn't lying about this.

However, serial killers, as we have noted, are not always reliable narrators. They can never quite be trusted - especially with their own story. History of a Drowning Boy, while interesting and littered with fresh details about Nilsen's life, can not be entirely trusted. Some of Nilsen's embellishments (like strangling animals - despite the act that he was famously an animal lover) feel suspicious. We are supposed to believe that Nilsen has somehow remembered a lot of stuff in prison that he forgot to tell Brian Masters.

All who met Dennis Nilsen said he was a dull and dour man in real life. These qualities come through in his writing. Nilsen is often tedious company when stretched out over 386 pages. Nilsen seems to think that every detail of his life (however trivial and mundane) has somehow been rendered fascinating because of his later infamy. That is most assuredly not the case though. There is unavoidably something quite tasteless about History of a Drowning Boy. Should serial killers really be allowed to write nostalgic memoirs as if they are normal celebrities like Terry Wogan? Ultimately it will be up to readers and those interested in true crime to decide for themselves.

For a time, Nilsen was considered to be the most prolific serial killer in British history. This changed when Harold Shipman came along. Dennis Nilsen is probably the second most famous Scottish serial killer. Ian Brady would probably edge out Nilsen for the top position. Dennis Nilsen may not actually even be the most prolific Scottish serial killer. It is possible that Peter Manuel and Peter Tobin might potentially have killed more people. This all all unverified though and not proven. It is still open to question how many of Dennis Nilsen's alleged unverified victims were real or not. In 2018, it was estimated that England had produced 145 serial killers in its history. Radford University's 2018 data estimated that Scotland had produced 15 serial killers.

Serial killers today are at a low level compared to the 1970s and 1980s. One theory for this is that the police have more technology at their disposal now and are simply better at catching murderers than they used to be. One other theory as to why serial killer murders are not as common as they used to be is that modern society is less risk adverse than it was in the 1970s and 1980s. People and (especially) teenagers and children tend to stay home (where they have social media and ample entertainment technology) more than they used to and are more clued up about danger. People also have mobile phones too so are always in contact and easy to trace.

If he was around today, Dennis Nilsen would most likely have been caught a lot sooner. The complaints made against him by gay men would have been investigated and it seems very likely that Nilsen would have been picked up on CCTV with many of his victims before he killed them. Nilsen was very much a product of his era in this respect. The attitudes and technology of the time in which he lived made it easier for him to be a killer.

Studies have shown that serial killers, as a collective, do not conform to any one stereotype. The come from all sorts of backgrounds - just like us. The chances of you walking past a serial killer in the street are slim. There really aren't that many of them compared to the general population. Dennis Nilsen was a very plain sight sort of killer. He worked in an office and never gave off an obviously alarming aura to work colleagues or even his victims. It seems it was only a few police colleagues who ever seemed to sense there was something potentially dark and dangerous about Dennis Nilsen.

The Dennis Nilsen case is ongoing. Even today, the police continue to try and identify unknown victims and welcome anyone who might have fresh information or suspect that Nilsen might have killed one of their relatives. There are, sadly, victims of Dennis Nilsen who will probably never be identified. As Dennis Nilsen once said - "If I had been arrested at sixty-five years of age there might have been thousands of bodies behind me."

Like many serial killers, Dennis Nilsen went to his grave with secrets. The story of Dennis Nilsen is one of the grimmest and most bizarre chapters in British criminal history. It is impossible to ever really explain how Dennis Nilsen came to be and why he did the things that he did. All we can say is that his strange fascination with death ultimately had tragic consequences. He was a truly strange and disturbing man. As Dennis Nilsen once wrote in prison - 'I lived with you and among you all.'